Lorenzo the Magnificent

HUGH ROSS WILLIAMSON

Lorenzo the Magnificent

MICHAEL JOSEPH

This book was devised and produced by
Park and Roche Establishment, Schaan

Copyright © 1974 by Hugh Ross Williamson
All rights reserved
First published in Great Britain in 1974 by
Michael Joseph Ltd, 52 Bedford Square, London WC1

Designed by Crispin Fisher
Picture research: Iconoscope, Florence
Printed by Amilcare Pizzi, Milano, Italy

ISBN 0 7181 1204 0

Jacket: *from Vasari's portrait of Lorenzo the Magnificent.*

Endpaper: *View of Florence in about 1470: anonymous engraving from* Della Catena.

Half-title: *Medal of Lorenzo the Magnificent by Niccolo Fiorentino.*

Title-page: *The Ponte S. Trinita over the river Arno in Florence.*

Contents

List of colour plates

Time mocks us gently when its silver smoke
Slips from the terraced olives.

Then we see
The calyx of the lily-tower; a dome
Lifted to be the heart of Tuscany;
And hear the steel of Ghibelline and Guelph
Clash in a city-state of Italy;
Or, in their muted thunder, Machiavel,
Savonarola, and the Medici.

All centuries renascent till light haze
Thickens beside the Arno.
History,
In high October, blurs before our gaze
Who look on Florence from Fiesole.

J. C. TREWIN: *From the Hill*

To Anthea, but for whom . . .

Foreword

Il Magnifico was not a title. It was a conventional courtesy, indiscriminately applied to eminent men. Renaissance Italy bristled with Magnificoes. Machiavelli, for instance, dedicated his treatise on statecraft, *The Prince*, to a Lorenzo *Il Magnifico* who was not our Lorenzo the Magnificent, but his weak, unpleasant grandson, the Duke of Urbino. And it is perhaps the best tribute to the greatness of the Lorenzo di Piero de' Medici, private citizen of Florence, who was born on New Year's Day, 1449, and died on Passion Sunday, 1492, that the appellation 'Lorenzo the Magnificent' was spontaneously awarded by his contemporaries and remains uniquely his in history.

'Even in his childhood', one of his earliest Florentine biographers noted, 'Lorenzo appears to have laid the foundation of his glory and his fame by which he obtained the appellations of *Magnificent* and *Magnanimous* by universal consent, for he displayed great liberality towards all and particularly towards the poor, so that nothing affected him more than the miseries of others and he found nothing more distressing than depressed and afflicted worth.'

He was hardly out of his boyhood when the ruler of Sicily, hearing of his love of fine horses, sent him one as a gift. Lorenzo acknowledged it by sending back presents worth three or four times that of the horse. When his tutor remonstrated with him for over-generosity, Lorenzo replied that there was nothing so glorious as to outdo all men in generosity. That was the true royalty.

The nickname which his tutor gave him, *Figlio del Sole*, Son of the Sun, would be, some think, a more appropriate title than *Il Magnifico* and certainly the uniqueness and omnipotence of the sun in all its aspects might well denote one for whom it has been rightly claimed that probably no other man in the history of the world had such great talents in so many directions. 'In statesmanlike insight and judgment; in political wisdom and promptness of decision; in power of influencing men; in profound knowledge of ancient classical authors; as a poet and writer who bore a principal part in the development of the Italian language; in artistic and critical knowledge of the various branches of art; in knowledge of agriculture, the life and needs of the people and country pursuits: in all these different directions, Lorenzo was eminent.' Thus, quietly and factually, an English writer at the beginning of this century, sums up Lorenzo's achievement, agreeing with the contemporary judgment of Machiavelli: 'Though noticeably without military ability, he yet conducted several wars to a successful conclusion by his diplomacy. He was the greatest patron of literature and art that any prince has ever been, and he won the people by his liberality and other popular qualities. By his political talents he made Florence the leading state of Italy and by his other qualities he made her the intellectual, artistic and fashionable centre of Italy.'

However, in the four centuries between these two judgments Lorenzo was consistently denigrated. He was a traitor who robbed Florence of her liberty, a tyrant who destroyed the Republic, a sybarite who set out to debauch his fellow-citizens so that he might the more easily enslave them, an enemy of the Church from the point-of-view of his Catholic detractors and a faithful son of it according to his more numerous Protestant critics, an avaricious banker who ruined Florentine finance in his own personal interests, a facile versifier who supplied the people with obscene songs and a patron of artists who painted lewd pictures.

The peak of such vilification is reached, it seems to me, paradoxically, not in an attack on him but in the liberal Sismondi's defence of the Pope's attempt, in the political interests of one of his illegitimate sons, to have Lorenzo assassinated by two priests while he had bared his head at the Elevation of the Host at Mass. On this episode, which surely represents the ultimate moment of corruption in the history of the Church, Sismondi comments that the Pope, although a corrupt man had 'a certain elevation of sentiment; he cared for the independence of Italy'.

Today, fortunately, the climate of opinion which made misjudgments of Lorenzo possible has been largely dissipated. Our greater understanding of the inter-relation of finance and politics makes such catch-words as 'representative democracy' and 'political liberty' acknowledged irrelevancies in estimating the actual quality of the life and freedom of the subject. Lorenzo's unique experiment – government of a Republic through an oligarchy by the wealthiest private citizen in the state who had been trained by his father and grandfather and who, possessing everything he could want, was devoid of any ambition for himself – may seem the nearest approach to a perfect solution. Certainly, in practice, the citizen of no state in Europe has ever been so free, so civilised, so contented and so prosperous as the Florentine during the Golden Age of Lorenzo the Magnificent. His detractors judge themselves, not him.

In addition to the outgrowing of the misleading eighteenth-, nineteenth- and twentieth-century myths of 'progress', 'liberalism' and 'democracy', there has been another change of intellectual climate which makes it easier to see Lorenzo as he was.

Scholars, of course, have always allowed for his praise and practice of Platonic love and appreciated the meaning of the annual performance by Lorenzo and his intimates of the *Symposium* on Plato's birthday. But popular works have tended to ignore or deliberately misinterpret it and to invent in its place supposed feminine 'romantic attachments'. He did, of course, undergo a marriage of convenience arranged for him by his parents and raise a family for the safeguarding of the succession. He disliked his wife, who was his social superior – she was an Orsini of Rome – and she quarrelled with his enduring lover, the poet Angelo Poliziano, who, five years his junior, lived in the Medici household from the age of ten and in whose arms Lorenzo died nearly thirty years later. It is probable that Lorenzo was also the lover of the young Michelangelo who was his last and greatest protégé.

The sexual atmosphere of Florence is best epitomised by the fact that the notably unattractive Dominican fanatic, Girolamo Savonarola gained his greatest popularity with the mob by denouncing Florence as the centre of sodomy in Italy and vehemently demanding that homosexuals should be publicly stoned and then burnt alive in the Piazza della Signoria – where he himself, six years after Lorenzo's death, was hanged and his body thrown to the flames.

Lorenzo himself had no particular beauty. In bodily gifts, it was said, Nature had proved herself a stepmother to him. His sight was weak, his voice harsh, his nose curiously shaped (*depresso*) and without a sense of smell. He had an olive complexion and was only a little above middle height. The weakness in his legs which made him prefer horsemanship to any other recreation, was in large measure due to the hereditary gout which killed his father, Piero 'the Gouty' and was eventually to kill him. But his personality triumphed over all obstacles. His charm was irresistible.

A natural demand by any reader, when the subject of a biography is a man of another nation, is for a rough guide to period. As Lorenzo lived at a watershed of history, it is perhaps most useful to note that he was four years old when Constantinople fell to the Turks and the riches of the Greek inheritance in the east were scattered over the west. Lorenzo's grandfather, Cosmo, had already made of Florence the ideal vessel to catch and drain the beneficent flood, so that the Renaissance naturally had its flowering there. Classical

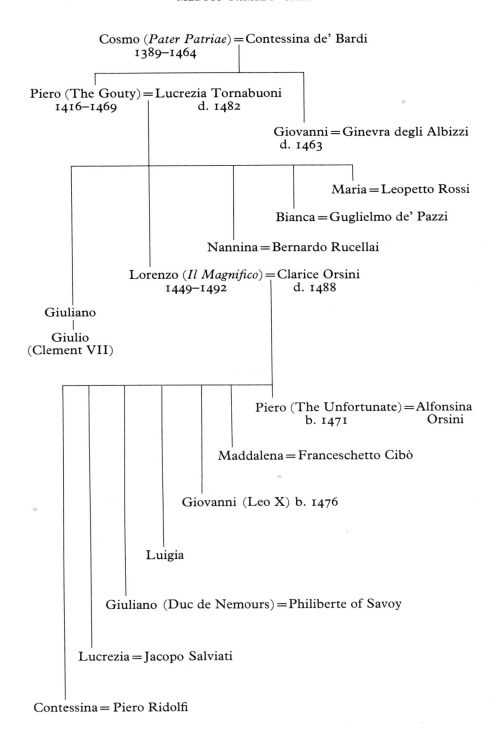

Cosmo (*Pater Patriae*) = Contessina de' Bardi
1389–1464

Piero (The Gouty) = Lucrezia Tornabuoni
1416–1469   d. 1482

Giovanni = Ginevra degli Albizzi
d. 1463

Maria = Leopetto Rossi

Bianca = Guglielmo de' Pazzi

Nannina = Bernardo Rucellai

Lorenzo (*Il Magnifico*) = Clarice Orsini
1449–1492   d. 1488

Giuliano

Giulio
(Clement VII)

Piero (The Unfortunate) = Alfonsina
b. 1471   Orsini

Maddalena = Franceschetto Cibò

Giovanni (Leo X) b. 1476

Luigia

Giuliano (Duc de Nemours) = Philiberte of Savoy

Lucrezia = Jacopo Salviati

Contessina = Piero Ridolfi

influence had, of course, been felt before then and about ten years before Lorenzo's birth, the great sculptor, Donatello, had made for Cosmo a statue of *David* to adorn the *cortile* of his new mansion in which Lorenzo was born and brought up. This was the first isolated nude statue that had been made for a thousand years and this 'remarkable innovation' (as Lord Balcarres calls it) was a domestic familiarity to Lorenzo from his nursery days.

To see Lorenzo in relation to England, it is easy to remember that it was eventually his favourite son, Pope Leo X, who excommunicated Luther (Savonarola's statue quite properly stands at the foot of Luther's memorial at Worms) and Lorenzo's nephew, Pope Clement VII, who, by refusing to allow King Henry VIII to divorce Catherine of Aragon, precipitated England into Protestantism.

Lorenzo's own lifetime corresponds for the major part with the English Wars of the Roses and the rule of the Yorkists (whom he financed). It is not of particular importance, though it may be of some interest, that his financial connection with England provided one of the more disastrous episodes of his banking experience. In addition to lending to the White Rose cause in general, the Medici bank in London financed the 'King-Maker' Warwick, at whose death they had to shoulder one of the overdrafts of all time. To make matters worse, Lorenzo's agent in London, Gherardo Canigiani, married an heiress, Dame Elizabeth Stockton, changed his name and became a naturalised Englishman and when Lorenzo sent the honest Christopher Spini to London to straighten things out, had him thrown into prison, with the result that the Florence bank was forced to repay 51,533 florins borrowed from Bruges before the London business could be closed down.

The businessman in Lorenzo is not of particular importance, if only because, however indifferently he exercised that skill, his father and grandfather had laid the foundation of the Medici fortune so well that, as the richest man in Europe, Lorenzo could indulge his magnificent patronage to the limit without going bankrupt. But Florentine art and letters cannot be understood at all without an appreciation of Lorenzo's pre-eminence as a poet. It is too often forgotten by those who speak glibly of 'Petrarch and Dante' that 'Lorenzo and Poliziano' take a not unworthy place beside them. And conventional approval of Botticelli is seldom aware that his three masterpieces, the *Primavera*, the *Birth of Venus* and *Mars and Venus* are primarily illustrations of Poliziano's poem on the occasion of Lorenzo's brother's tournament, which the poet managed to make a paean of praise for *Il Magnifico*.

But it is at an earlier tournament – his own – that he still seems most alive, though his diary-note (quoted on p. 88) is pedestrian enough.

But, through other eyes, we may enjoy this glimpse of the youth of nineteen, on the eve of power but with nearly half his life-span spent, astride a nonpareil white charger, caparisoned in his colours of red and white, and across his breast a broad silk scarf, embroidered with roses, some in bud, some full-blown, some fading, and with his motto *Le Temps Revient* picked out in pearls.

Here is truly the Renaissance and we seem to hear the strains of Lorenzo's most famous song which rang through Europe bidding youth to gather roses while it could –

> *Quant'è bella giovinezza,*
> *Che si fugge tuttavia!*
> *Chi vuol esser lieto, sia :*
> *Di doman non c'è certezza.*

The blazons of the Medici family and the Guild of Wool on the lid of the tomb of Guccio de' Medici, gonfalonier of Florence in 1299.

Florence and the Medici

As from the protecting hills one looks down on Florence, the red dome of the Cathedral of St Mary of the Flowers and the green and white marble of Giotto's campanile beside it distract the eye from the octagonal Baptistery which is, in Ruskin's phrase, 'the central building of European Christianity'.

Where this now stands was once the Temple of Mars, the tutelary god of the City of Flowers when it was Florentia, a town of the Roman Empire with its forum and baths and temples and amphitheatre and aqueduct and straight, symmetrical streets. When it became Christianised, some time before the edict of Constantine in 313 legalised the new faith, it took as its patron St John the Baptist and stowed away the statue of Mars in a tower near the river, while it turned his temple into the Baptistery, whose shape made it almost defiantly Christian – for the octagon was symbolic of Christ's victory over death, six sides betokening the six days of the material creation, the seventh the day on which God rested from His work and the eighth the Resurrection which inaugurated the new, spiritual creation.

But Mars was not altogether banished from the people's minds. In the fifth century the 'beloved sheep-fold of St John', as Dante called it, was destroyed by the barbarian hordes from the east and the hidden statue of the God of War fell into the river. The Florentines had enough respect – or fear – to rescue it from the Arno and set it up on a pillar at the north entrance of the Ponte Vecchio, believing that otherwise their city would never be re-built. Later, they came to attribute their interminable strife to the offended

Opposite: *View of Florence from the Viale dei Colli: in the centre is the Cathedral of Santa Maria del Fiore, surmounted on the left by Giotto's campanile, on the right by Brunelleschi's dome.*

dignity of their one-time patron. As Dante put it in the *Inferno*:

> *Io fui della cità che nel Batista*
> *Mutò 'l primo patrono : ond' ei per questo*
> *Sempre con l'arte sua la farà trista*
> *E se non fosse che in sul passo d' Arno*
> *Rimane ancor di lui alcuna vista*
> *Quei cittadin, che poi la rifondarno*
> *Sopra il cener che d'Attila rimase*
> *Avrebber fatto lavorare indarno.*

I was of the city that changed its first patron for the Baptist on which account he with his art will always make it sorrowful; and were it not that at the passage of the Arno there still remains some semblance of him, those citizens who afterwards rebuilt it on the ashes left by Attila would have laboured in vain.

The entanglement of the two patrons, symbolic of a continuing dichotomy, was continued by a famous race, held annually on June 24, St John the Baptist's Day, from the column of Mars at the Ponte Vecchio to the Baptistery; and when the column was eventually removed on account of a murder which took place there on Easter Day 1215 which led to a fifty-two-year blood-feud it was transferred to the Baptistery, facing the High Altar, its white channelled marble contrasting almost militantly with the Sardinian granite of the other columns.

But the strange duality was still not at an end. Mars, transformed into the affectionate diminutive, *Il Marzocco*, a seated lion holding a shield, bearing as its device Our Lady's flower, the lily, became the heraldic emblem of Florence, immortalised by Donatello's sculpture; and those who were vanquished in war by the Florentines were required to do homage to it by kissing its hind-quarters.

The murder which took place at the foot of the Mars column in 1215 divided the city into Guelfs and Ghibellines, which was the basis of all subsequent groupings. Originally the Guelfs had been the supporters of the Pope and the Ghibellines the partisans of the Emperor in the centuries-long Papal-Imperial struggle, but the names gradually came to have as little relevance to their origins as, in English politics, Whig and Tory had to a Scottish covenanter and an Irish kern. What significance they retained was as useful labels for antagonistic social and political ideals. The Imperialists

Opposite: *The Palazzo Publico in Florence, official residence of the Signori, the leaders of the Guilds.*

originally were, in the main, Teutonic nobles living in castles outside the city while the Papalists tended to be citizens of pure Latin stock. Thus Ghibellinism came to mean, on the whole, feudal domination by an alien caste, Guelfism a measure of municipal independence and the control of the city-state by native Italian citizens.

It was a personal matter that introduced the division into Florence. The two most powerful houses at the beginning of the thirteenth century were the Buondelmonti and the Amidei. A marriage had been arranged to bind them closely together when suddenly the Buondelmonte bridegroom-to-be jilted his Amidei intended for the beautiful daughter of another house, the Donati. The Amidei, aided by their partisans, the Uberti, thereupon arranged the murder of the defaulting bridegroom.

An historian of Florence thus recorded it: 'On Easter Day the conspirators gathered together in the house of the Amidei, and Messer Buondelmonte coming from the other side of the Arno, bravely dressed in new garments white all over, and riding a white palfrey, when he reached the foot of the Ponte Vecchio on this side, just at the base of the pillar where stood the statue of Mars, the said Messer Buondelmonte was thrown from his horse on the ground by Schiatti degli Uberti and set on and stabbed by Lambertuccio degli Amidei and his throat cut and an end made of him.

'Thereupon the city rushed to arms in an uproar; and the death of Messer Buondelmonte was the cause and beginning of the accursed Guelf and Ghibelline parties in Florence, for all the families of the nobles and other citizens took sides and some held with the Buondelmonti, who joined the Guelph party and became its leaders, and some with the Uberti who became the leaders of the Ghibellines.'

For over half a century, the conflict raged. At one point the Ghibellines, with the help of the Emperor Frederick II, expelled the Guelfs from the city and razed their houses to the ground. On the Emperor's death shortly afterwards, the Guelf came back, threw out the more militant Ghibellines and changed the arms of Florence from a white lily on a red ground to a red lily on a white ground. The remaining Ghibellines, clinging to their white lily, bided their time and conspired with Manfred to overthrow the Guelf government, but the Florentines rose in arms against them, drove them out of the city and demolished their houses. They fled to Siena and, when the Florentines were ill-advised enough to attack it, cut them to pieces in a victory so sweeping that before very long, according to the old chronicler, 'There remained neither town nor castle, small or great, throughout Tuscany, but was subject to the Ghibellines.'

Opposite: *Donatello's sculpture* Il Marzocco.

The annual horse-race from the Ponte Vecchio to the Baptistery: panel painted by Jacopo Franchi in the fifteenth century.

Again the balance shifted and the Florentine Guelfs, 'feeling themselves strong again', applied for help to Charles of Anjou who sent them eight hundred French horsemen, which arrived before Florence on Easter Day, 1267, exactly fifty-two years after the start of the feud and the Ghibellines 'departed out of Florence without stroke of sword' and never returned.

Thirteen years later, in 1280, is the first mention of the family which was to bring Florence to her golden age, when a certain Ugo de' Medici was banished for his infraction of the peace.

The main importance of these years which saw the eventual triumph of the Guelf ideal was however the forging of a constitution which was supposed to guarantee a people's republic.

The Florentine's passion for liberty, rooted in the ideals of Greece and Rome, was what immediately distinguished him from other Italians. Liberty was considered the highest good and was interpreted as meaning both freedom from foreign domination and a republican rule under which every class had equal opportunities. In pursuit of this impossibility the Florentines (who as their greatest contemporary historian, Guicciardini, acidly observed, combined a passion for equality with a desire of each family to be first in the city) devised a constitution of such unworkable complexity that it proved an

22

irresistible invitation to bribery and led eventually to the tyranny of the rich, providing, indeed, the classic example of the dictum that democracy is merely the mask for plutocracy. That the despots happened to be the great banking family of the Medici, whose greatest member, Lorenzo the Magnificent, was at pains to stress, at the height of his power when he spoke as an equal to the crowned heads of Europe, that he was only a simple citizen, merely emphasised the strength of the egalitarian myth.

The executive government of Florence was placed in the hands of four distinct and different people or bodies of people, each subject to the advice of one or more deliberative councils. They were: twelve 'Good Men' (*Buoniuomini*), who held office for no more than two months, assisted by a council of a hundred; the Captain of the People (*Capitano del Popolo*), assisted by, first, eighty members of the great Guilds and, secondly, a general council of three hundred citizens, drawn from each division (*sesto*) of Florence; the Podestà, a *foreign* knight or prince, learned in the law, appointed annually to administer civil and criminal justice, who was advised by ninety members of the Council of the Podestà, as well as the Council of the Commune, a mixed body of a hundred and twenty nobles and commoners; and, finally, the *Parte Guelfa*, a sort of mediaeval Tammany Hall, operating behind the scenes in secret and pulling all the political strings. It consisted of six *Capitani*, three nobles and three representatives of the people.

Towards the end of the thirteenth century, a change was made to bring the appearance of the government more into line with the realities of power, which was now entrusted to the leaders of the principal Guilds – the *Priori* of the *Arti* – who, to add to their dignity, were called *Signori* and given an official residence in the Palazzo Publico, with all the paraphernalia of staff and officers. The *Signoria* attached to itself a Gonfalonier of Justice, who had at his disposal a thousand armed men, so that when, at the bidding of the *Capitano del Popolo* he raised the gonfalon, the bell in the Lion's Tower would summon the waiting militia to enforce what was called 'obedience to lawful authority' but what in fact was usually some new and oppressive enactment forced by a venal *Signoria* controlled by the *Parte Guelfa* and the wealthiest of the *Priori* on a disenfranchised and discontented working class, unorganised and without any share whatever in political power.

The lowest of the low were, in the main, responsible for acclaiming a French adventurer, Walter de Brienne, Duke of Athens, who had been appointed generalissimo of the Florentine forces in a war against Lucca, as their prince for life. He was a worthless character who, after a year's exercise of sovereign power, alienated all classes in the state. A general rising against him, in which the Medici family played an important part, was organised and on July 26,

1343, his government was overthrown and the Duke himself ignominiously expelled.

The day was St Anne's Day which thereafter became a red-letter day in the Florentine calendar, while in art the saint began to appear conspicuously as the protectress of the Florentine Republic. Indeed it is probable that the present day's *Festa delle Rificolone*, when children parade through the city with lighted lanterns on the eve of Our Lady's Birthday, was originally a tribute to St Anne, the mother of Our Lady; and the Masolino-Masaccio painting of St Anne with the Virgin and Child, where Christ's grandmother magnificently dominates the group, leaves no doubt of contemporary Florentine feeling of her importance.

The saints were prominent in the life of mediaeval Florence, for each of the trade-guilds (*Arti*) had its patron among them and honoured him not only by processions and pageants on his feast day but by making themselves responsible for the upkeep and beautification of the churches dedicated to him. The Orsanmichele, where in the eighth century an oratory, San Michele in Orto – St Michael in the garden – had stood and later been replaced by a granary until, six years before the expulsion of the Duke of Athens, a new

The Ponte Vecchio over the river Arno, starting-point of an annual horse-race held on St John the Baptist's Day.

and splendid building arose which combined uniquely a church and a market hall, was the pride of the Guilds, intended to exhibit their wealth and magnificence. Each niche and pillar was adopted and maintained by one of the Guilds, with the intention that Mass should be said on a portable altar before each one at the appropriate times. The younger Florentine sculptors were commissioned to fashion statues of the patron saints of the Guilds with the result that, as one writer has put it, 'It was as if the preceding almost blank forty years of sculpture in Florence were a predestined wait for Nanni di Banco, Ghiberti and Donatello, the miraculous generation which came of age between 1406 and 1426'. The finest, as well as the most famous, of them was Donatello's St George, patron saint of the Swordmakers and Armourers (*Arte dei Spadia e Coruzzi*) but the originals of the earliest of them, those belonging to the two most powerful and inter-related Guilds, the native wool trade and the foreign cloth merchants, are lost and replaced by later versions of St Stephen and St John the Baptist.

Most important of the seven Greater Guilds (*Arti Maggiori*) were the four connected with the cloth and woollen trade which was the basis of the city's prosperity. The two most venerable, stretching back to at least the ninth century were the Guild of Wool (*Arte della Lana*) and the Guild of Foreign Merchants (*Arte di Calimala*), with which were associated the Guild of Bankers (*Arte del Cambio*), so essential for the financing of a Europe-wide trade and the Guild of Silk (*Arte della Seta*). Two other of the seven whose skills were required by the commercial colossus were the Physicians and Druggists (*Medici e Speziali*), because of their specialised knowledge of drugs and chemicals used in the preparation and dyeing of the cloth and the Advocates (*Giudici e Notai*), essential for the framing of foreign contracts and adjudicating between the Guilds themselves.

Five years before the expulsion of the Duke of Athens, the Calimala (whose name was supposed to derive from the Greek and signify 'pure fleece'), had more than two hundred workshops (*botteghe*), employed thirty thousand workmen, supplied between seventy and eighty thousand pieces of cloth at the price of over a million golden florins, and had its representatives in France, Flanders and England. At the end of the thirteenth century Florentine agents in London, dealing with as many as two hundred abbeys and convents, bought up the wool for several years in advance. The guildhall of the Calimala, which had as its device an eagle of gold holding a ball of wool, adjoined Orsanmichele. At the corner of the Via Calimala and the Old Market was the University or residence of the Physicians and, near it, the hall of the Bankers.

This quarter of Florence, the site of the Capitol in pre-Christian times, was the pride of the citizens and the centre of the great houses of the nobility,

Walter de Briennes, Duke of Athens, was expelled from Florence after an uprising against him on July 26, 1343: this was St Anne's Day, and this allegorical part of an anonymous fresco shows St Anne herself driving out the worthless and unpopular generalissimo.

27

A golden Florentine florin of about 1416. During Lorenzo's lifetime Florence was the most flourishing state in Europe and the golden florin had become the general standard of value on the Continent. It continued to hold its credit in Europe until 1530. It weighed 72 grains of gold and represented twelve francs. The equivalent value in English money at the beginning of the twentieth century was about £2.

where they spent the six months of the year they did not spend at their villas in the hills. Antonio Pucci in a long topographical poem described the piazza as it appeared in the first part of the fourteenth century:

The Old Market provides food for all the world
And carries off the prize from every other piazza.
Such is the grandeur of this market
That it has four churches at the four corners
And at every corner are two streets.
Physicians dwell around for every ill,
And here are linen cloths, and flax merchants,
Pork vendors and apothecaries.
And here also are the great exchanges,
And many money-changers may be counted,
Since their merchandise is most demanded;
Such as lenders and dealers in old articles,
Tables of ready-money, and dice players,
Of every sort that each may carry on his trade.

> *Mercato Vecchio al mondo è alimento*
> *Ed al ogni altra piazza il pregio serra.*
> *La dignità di mercato son queste*
> *Ch' ha quattro chiese ne suoi quattro canti*
> *Ed ogni canto ha due vie manifesti.*
> *Medici v' ha d'intorno a tutti mali,*
> *Ed avvi panni, lini, e linaioli,*
> *V' ha pizzicagnoli e v' ha speziali.*
> *E sempre quivi ha gran Baratteria*
> *E c' ha contar molti baratterieri*
> *Perchè v' ha più da lor mercatanzia;*
> *Cio è di prestatori e rigattioro*
> *Tavole di contanti e dadaiouli*
> *D' ogni ragion che farne a lor mestier.*

The arms of the Cambio were a red field bearing golden coins, presumably the golden florins – *Fiorno d'oro* – which celebrated the city's name. The arms of the Medici family, the origin of which is entirely unknown, are red discs on a golden field. Originally there were eleven of them, but after becoming nine and then seven they were eventually reduced by Lorenzo the Magnificent to six – five red and one blue. The blue one bore the lily of France (quite different from the Florentine *giglio* which is an iris) which was granted to Lorenzo's father by King Louis XI as a token of the esteem in which he held him. It is possible that the arms were adopted by the Medici, who were a great people for hidden heraldic devices, as a mere inversion of those of the Cambio.

On the other hand, as the discs are known as balls (*palle*), it is equally possible that they were originally meant for apothecary's pills and that the Medici's Guild was the *Arte della Medici* – a theory supported by the fact that the founder of the greatness of their house, the Pater Patriae, Cosmo, was named after St Cosmas, the Arabian physician who with his twin brother St Damian, had been the patron saint of doctors since the fourth century and was considered of sufficient inportance to be named – as they still are – in the Canon of the Mass. Also the saints were usually included in pictures painted for him or in his honour. However, as Cosmas and Damian were usually venerated under the sobriquet of 'the moneyless ones' because they refused to take any remuneration from their patients, a refusal which weighed heavily in the scales of sanctity, it is possible that the Medici family noticed a certain incompatibility of outlook and found coins of the Cambio a more appropriate emblem. They were definitely of the *Popolo Grasso* – 'the fat people' – the wealthy, prosperous commercial men, members of the *Arti Maggiori*, from whom, in the next generation or two, the great merchant-princes were to rise.

At the other end of the social scale were the *Ciompi*, the unorganised working classes, without any share of political power, ineligible for membership of the seven major or the fourteen minor Guilds, and equally oppressed whatever the complexion of the government. The later years of the fourteenth century saw all over Europe violent movements of the non-privileged masses, all asserting the equality of men and demanding higher wages and better working conditions. The most famous and the most violent were the Peasants' Revolt, led by Wat Tyler, in England and the Jacquerie, led by Etienne Marcel, in France. With them must be classed, though it was on a smaller and less sanguinary scale, the *Ciompi* revolt in Florence, led by Michele di Lando, a wool-comber, in 1378. Michele set up a government which revised the constitution and made three new Guilds for the workers; but in 1381 it was overthrown and power was resumed by the burghers of the Greater Guilds, which meant in practice an oligarchy in the hands of the powerful Albizzi family.

It was at this point that the Medici family began to emerge as challengers of the Albizzi hegemony and, as far as commercial prudence allowed, as champions of a sort of the *popolani* against the *grandi*. Their representative was Giovanni, known as 'di Bicci', a nickname bestowed on his father,

Opposite: *A sixteenth-century sculpted and painted wood blazon of the Medici family: the number of palles was reduced to six by Lorenzo the Magnificent: the blue palle bears the lily of France.*

Overleaf: *Domenico de Michelino's fresco in the Cathedral shows the poet Dante holding a copy of his* Commedia *which sheds its light upon the city of Florence.*

DVX·ALESADER·P·M·

AVE · MARIA · GRA · PLENA · DOMINVS · TECVM · BEDICTA · TV

Averado, who had spent his life carefully shunning publicity while he single-mindedly devoted himself to amassing a fortune by the family business of banking.

The money-trade, as it may be called, was, even more than wool and cloth and silk, the reason for Florence's European fame from the twelfth century and characteristically the first known bill of exchange, in 1199, was a Florentine invention. All the furniture that was required by a member of the *Arte del Cambio* was a table covered with green cloth – *tavola di contanti* – a purse of money, and an accounts book, for which reason the Guild was popularly known as 'the Company of the Table'. Through the lower reaches of money-lending, the ancestors of Averado 'di Bicci' climbed to the heights of international banking, so that Averado was able to pass on to his son, Giovanni 'di Bicci' a fortune which made him virtually the money-master of Italy, capable of effecting a financial crisis in almost any quarter where it suited him. The ramifications of his banking business extended to the Levant in the east and to England in the north. In Florence itself, almost every important citizen was either Giovanni's client or his debtor and he won the approval of the lower classes by a display of nicely calculated generosities.

That Averado was given the nickname of 'Bicci' and that Giovanni inherited it is of considerable relevance to the understanding of the Medici, for the original Buiamonte de' Bicci was the notorious Florentine banker whom Dante in his *Inferno* had set in the desert of burning sand and rain of fire, sitting with his eyes fixed on the purse hanging round his neck – a usurer punished as one who had done violence to Nature and Art.

Since the teaching of the mediaeval Church on the subject of usury is today almost entirely forgotten and as, in the context of the Medici, it is a veritable crux of comprehension, a reminder of it may be permissible. Dorothy Sayers in her commentary on the *Inferno* has put it simply: 'There are only two sources of real wealth – Nature and Art, or, as we should put it, Natural Resources and the Labour of Man. The buying and selling of money as though it were a commodity creates only a spurious wealth, and results in injury to the earth (Nature) and in the exploitation of labour (Art). The attitude to men and things which this implies is a kind of blasphemy; since Art derives from Nature, as Nature derives from God, so that contempt of them is contempt of Him.'

Opposite: *The inclusion of St Anne standing behind the Virgin in Masolino and Masaccio's painting is an indication of her importance to the Florentines.*

Overleaf left: *Donatello's statue of St George, patron saint of the Guild of Swordmakers and Armourers, who commissioned the work.*

35

And though 'Art' has here the mediaeval significance of all honest work – the Guilds are the *Arti* – it may also in Dante's mind have the more limited meaning which modernity attaches to the word, as when the poet Virgil says to the poet Dante: 'Your art is, as it were, the grand-child of God' (*vostr' arte a Dio quasi è nipote*).

In any case, the great Medici passionate encouragement of 'Art' in both senses, as well as their almost disproportionate devotion to church-building and endowment and restoration, which might be considered (and possibly was in fact) 'for the greater glory of God', suggests that the 'Bicci' taunt had bitten deep. It is even arguable that the youthful repudiation of Christianity by Lorenzo the Magnificent (who was born only twenty years after his great-grandfather, Giovanni 'di Bicci' died) was due in part to his clear-minded perception that his creed and his craft were contrarieties.

It is certain, however, that if the name of Medici today calls up the admired image of a munificent art-patron, its immediate association in the fourteenth century was with usury, the besetting sin of Florence. The Jews, at this time when they were being expelled from England and France, were actually invited to settle in Florence on the understanding that they would not charge more than twenty per cent, in the hope that their competition would bring down the general level of interest.

In 1429, in the seventieth year of his age, Giovanni (di Bicci) de' Medici died and was succeeded in the headship of his house by his forty-year-old son, Cosmo, who was unencumbered by the insulting 'Bicci' sobriquet and lived to earn the honourable title, *Pater Patriae*, father of his country.

Giovanni di Bicci de' Medici : portrait by Bronzino.

The twin patron saints of
Cosmo de' Medici,
the third century physicians
Cosmas and Damian:
painting by Bicci di Lorenzo.

The Education of Lorenzo

Florence in the year 1400 was visited by a devastating plague which, as a climax to the foreign wars, the internal riots, the political upheavals, the food shortages, the inflation and the bankruptcies that had made the past forty years seem the most unfortunate in the Republic's history, spread superstitious terror among citizens of all classes. It was therefore decided, as a kind of votive offering to appease an angry deity, to provide two new bronze doors for the Baptistery, which had been allowed to fall into disgraceful disrepair since the first two doors had been hung in place, sixty or so years before; and, as their designer, Andrea Pisano, was now dead, to hold a competition, open to all Italians, to find a suitable designer. The expense was to be borne by the *Calimala* which as the largest Guild assumed responsibility for everything connected with the city's patron saint.

The official announcement of the competition, early in 1401, is now usually regarded as the beginning of the Renaissance of Italian art. The subject set was Abraham's sacrifice of Isaac, which, so Vasari explained 'was considered to be a good subject in which the masters could grapple with the difficulties of their art, because it comprises a landscape, figures both nude and draped, and animals, while the figures in the foreground might be made in full relief, those in the middle-distance in half-relief, and those in the background in bas-relief'. The seven sculptors – of which only three were Florentines – were given a year to complete a bronze panel of the size of those on the existing doors.

At the adjudication, the thirty-four judges soon reduced the competitors to two, both of them twenty-four-year-old Florentine goldsmiths, Lorenzo Ghiberti and Filippo Brunelleschi. As soon as Brunelleschi saw Ghiberti's panel, he withdrew from the contest, 'saying that it would be more shameful to dispute his rival's right to pre-eminence than generous to admit it'.

Whether or not this particular judgment was correct it was undoubtedly Brunelleschi who was the greater artist and the greater influence. As Vasari

In 1401 the largest Guild in Florence financed a competition to design two new bronze doors for the Baptistery. The subject set was Abraham's sacrifice of Isaac. These are the two models which were short-listed: on the left, Brunelleschi's, and, on the right, the design by Ghiberti in whose favour Brunelleschi withdrew from the competition.

41

wrote: 'It may be said that he was given by Heaven to invest architecture with new forms, after it had wandered astray for many centuries, during which the men of the time had expended much money to bad purpose in erecting buildings devoid of arrangement, in bad style, of sorry design, with the oddest notions, most ungraceful grace and worse ornament. It was Heaven's decree, after the world had been for so many years without a master mind and divine spirit that Filippo Brunelleschi should leave to the world the greatest and loftiest building, the finest of all the achievements of ancient and modern times, proving that the ability of the Tuscan artists though lost was not dead.'

When a century earlier, the building of the new cathedral was decided on, the *Signoria* instructed the architect that it 'should be designed so as to be worthy of a heart expanded to much greatness, corresponding to the noble city's soul, which is composed of the souls of all its citizens'. Now to Brunelleschi was entrusted the task of completing it and giving it its crowning glory, the octagonal red dome, the wonder of the age and still the largest double cupola in Europe.

Brunelleschi, too, was commissioned by the Medici to restore and rebuild their family church, San Lorenzo, originally founded by a pious Roman matron in 373; and when Cosmo, on the death of his father in 1429, decided to build a new family residence more appropriate to his importance as one who now owned banks in sixteen capital cities of Europe, including Paris, London, Bruges, Rome and Venice, he ordered Brunelleschi to draw up the plans. But the grandeur of the architect's conception alarmed him. It may be that they gave him warning of the dangerous hubristic implications of the intended change of residence. He rejected Brunelleschi's plans and engaged in his stead the younger Michelozzo Michelozzi.

Michelozzo was the pupil of Donatello, the greatest of Florentine sculptors who seemed intent on establishing a monopoly of the city's patron saint by producing over twenty different statues of St John the Baptist – as a child, as a youth, as a man, in relief, in bust and in full-length, in marble and in bronze. Donatello retained the services of Michelozzo in his studio because of his skill in working marble and casting bronze, but the younger man's real interest was in architecture, 'in planning and devising palaces, convents and houses and exercising his judgment in their arrangement'. In consequence

Opposite: *Self-portrait in bronze incorporated by Ghiberti on the* Door of Paradise *of the Baptistery.*

Overleaf: *Vasari's narrative painting shows Brunelleschi and Ghiberti presenting to Cosmo de' Medici a model of the new church of San Lorenzo in the presence of Donatello and Michelozzo: in the background, the church is being built.*

Michelozzo's design for a Medici palace was only a little less lordly than Brunelleschi's. Nor did it allow Cosmo to escape the consequences of indulging his dreams of grandeur.

The house was to be built in the widest street in Florence, the Via Larga, at the corner of a short street running down to the Church of San Lorenzo. It was to be large enough to house comfortably three generations and was to surpass anything of the kind hitherto seen – to be deliberately, in fact, a model of architectural art surpassing any other private dwelling, even a royal palace, in Europe. It was to display three distinct styles, the ground floor having the strength of a castle, the second storey being in the classic simplicity of Doric and the third the elaboration of Corinthian.

It was the first time that the style *rustica* used for the ground floor had been seen, though it soon became very popular. It consisted of large, rough-hewn blocks, straight from the quarry (or carefully carved to look as if they were) suitable for a fortress and with the same protective intention in a time and place so prolific of riots and risings. Michelozzo explained that he adopted it 'because it united an appearance of solidity and strength with the light and shadow so essential to beauty under the glare of Italian sun'. The style was prodigiously expensive and when the walls of the new building were of a sufficient height for it to be appreciated, Cosmo's many and powerful enemies decided that his latest venture might be utilised for his disadvantage and even for his downfall.

At the beginning of September 1433 a new *Signoria*, drawn by lot, was found to be composed overwhelmingly of supporters of Rinaldo degli Albizzi, the principal opponent of the Medici. On September 7 Cosmo was summoned by the Gonfalonier to present himself at the Palazzo della Signoria and answer the charge of scheming to exalt himself above the rank of an ordinary citizen (the worst possible charge in Florence). Among other things his new palace was cited as being too grand for a simple citizen and thus providing evidence of an ambition dangerous to the Republic.

In due course a sentence of banishment was passed by the aristocratically-minded *Signoria* and the Medici were expelled from Florence as 'being dangerous to the Republic by reason of their wealth and ambition'. They were escorted under guard to the frontier, Cosmo himself (voluntarily accompanied by Michelozzi) going to Venice.

Effectively to exile an international banker of Cosmo's importance was, of course, completely impossible. In Venice he had, in addition to many powerful friends and clients, a branch of his bank. His 'diversion and pastime'

Opposite: *Pontormo's portrait of Lorenzo's grandfather Cosmo de' Medici, who was temporarily exiled in 1433.*

might appear to be reading the classics in the new library which, at his expense, he ordered Michelozzo to design and build for the monastery of S Giorgio Maggiore, but he continued skilfully to 'fix' things in Florence. The next *Signoria*, drawn by lot in the following September was composed almost entirely of his creatures and at its invitation he returned in triumph to Florence on October 1, 1434 to rule the Republic in fact if not in name till his death, thirty years later.

The building of the Palazzo Medici was not completed till 1459, by which time Lorenzo, his eldest grandson, was ten years old, but as early as 1440, nine years before the future *Il Magnifico's* birth, Cosmo decided to live there with his family, consisting of his wife, Contessina de' Bardi, and their two sons, Piero, who was twenty-four at the time, and Giovanni, who was nineteen.

Piero was a chronic invalid, immobilised for days at a time by a crippling gout which gave him the nickname of *Il Gottoso*, the Gouty One. It grew worse with the years and prevented him from taking any active part in public affairs for increasingly long periods, while other ailments attacked his enfeebled constitution and made it probable that he would predecease his father. In consequence, it was natural for Cosmo to treat his younger son, Giovanni, more and more as if he were the heir.

Giovanni's good looks, his robust constitution and his intellectual grasp of political and economic problems suggested that he would fill admirably a rôle requiring a combination of capability in administration and an affability guaranteeing popularity with the plebs. Piero found what pleasure he had in life in conversation with and encouragement of artists and scholars and in making 'a collection of pictures, manuscripts, jewels, cameos, vases, bronzes, medallions and rare books without equal in Europe' as a visiting connoisseur described it. It was as if Cosmo's two sons had developed the two sides of his nature and were, in a sense, complementary to the continued leadership of the Medici; nor, since there was no jealousy between them, did it seem that they considered themselves in any other light. And Cosmo, in his choice of wives for them, did not ignore the differences. For Piero he chose Lucrezia Tornabuoni, one of the most accomplished women of the age, a poetess who had written, among other verse, a life of St John the Baptist in *terza rima*, a friend and patron of scholars and artists and a businesswoman who, on her own account, bought from the Republic the sulphur springs at Morba and turned the place into a flourishing health resort. As for Giovanni's wife, the important thing was her political affiliations and it was enough that she was

Opposite: *Brunelleschi's dome on the Cathedral of Santa Maria del Fiore.*

an Albizzi and that such a marriage would prevent any recrudescence of the fatal feud.

In 1440, there moved into the Palazzo Medici, which still required twenty years' work on it, Cosmo and his domestic-minded Contessina, his heir, Piero the Gouty, and his Lucrezia Tornabuoni, intent on the patronage of art and scholarship, and Giovanni, the hope of the Medici, as yet unmarried and his father's favourite.

The previous year, 1439, had seen the family at the height of its influence and fame. As Cosmo's personal guests there had come to Florence from Constantinople the Eastern Emperor, John Palaeologus accompanied by Joseph, Patriarch of Constantinople, and a large number of bishops and theologians of the Eastern Church. From Rome had come the Pope, Eugenius IV, with his train of cardinals, bishops and theologians of the Western Church. All the most learned men of West and East alike were to discuss, in a council convened beneath Brunelleschi's new dome, means of healing the schism between Rome and the Eastern Church and for protecting the city of Constantinople from the impending attack of the barbaric Turks.

In both its declared aims, the Council of Florence failed, though its ultimate result was to ensure that, in due time, Florence became 'the Athens of the West'. For the month of its sitting, the intellectual interchanges it provoked among the privileged and the familiarity with the customs and costumes of the East it initiated among the populace, ensured that when the dreadful day it had tried to prevent – the capture of Constantinople by the Turks – inevitably came, thirteen years later, the treasures of the pillaged Greek civilisation found their way first of all to Florence.

Among the citizens who gazed with wonder and curiosity at the magnificently attired visitors from the East as, on July 6, 1439, they made a solemn procession throughout the streets of Florence, led by the Emperor, the Patriarch and the Pope, was a twenty-year-old painter, Benozzo Gonzoli. He was attached to the studio of Fra Angelico, 'deservedly loved by his master' not only for his skill but because 'he worked hard, taking but little pleasure in other diversions'. To him Cosmo de' Medici entrusted the recording of the event in the glowing colours of fresco on the walls of the little chapel on the first floor of his new palace under the guise of *The Journey of the Magi*. The first Wise Man was the Emperor, John VIII, wearing, entwined with his turban, the peculiar crown of the Eastern Emperors of Rome, so different in shape from that which had been at that time adopted by all the sovereigns of Western Europe. The second Wise Man was the

Opposite: *The head of John Palaeologus, the Eastern Emperor, who attended the Council of Florence in 1439: detail from Gozzoli's* The Journey of the Magi.

Patriarch Joseph, an old man with a long white beard (who was in fact on the point of death and never returned to Constantinople) also wearing his distinctive crown, the ancient head-dress which the East had retained while their colleagues in the West, the Popes, had gradually altered it and allowed it to grow into a triple crown, the Tiara.

The third Wise Man should have been the Pope, Eugenius IV, but at the moment this presented some diplomatic difficulties. A fortnight earlier, during the sitting of the council, he had been officially deposed by a General Council of the Church, sitting at Basel, which proceeded to elect an inconsiderable mediocre Pope in his stead under the title of Felix V. As only posterity could decide which was Pope and which Anti-Pope, the presence of Eugenius in fresco might prove embarrassing.

How the problem was solved we have no means of knowing. In the fresco as it exists today the third Wise Man is Lorenzo the Magnificent, Cosmo's grandson, who was not born till 1449 and is shown as he appeared on a great occasion in 1469 – the spectacular tournament he held to celebrate his marriage. Benozzo Gozzoli was by that time fifty, but equally a spectator of the great event of 1469 as he had been of that of 1439. The most probable explanation is that he painted out the original third Wise Man and substituted Lorenzo. He had been careful in the 1439 procession to include himself among the followers of the Medici, his youthful freshness accentuated by the grave, bearded scholars walking on either side of him, and his identity proclaimed to every onlooker by his name written round his red hat.

The Medici themselves, as they were constituted in 1439, recognisably lead the procession following the Magi. Cosmo and his brother Lorenzo, both white-haired, though the elder was fifty and the younger forty-four, ride side by side, inseparable as they were in life, but with Lorenzo seated on a humble mule as became his self-effacement. He already occupied the house in the Via Larga next door to Cosmo's new palace and devoted himself entirely to the vast commercial interests of the family. Their 'Bicci' father had deliberately not made a will, leaving the brothers to make their agreed apportionment of his millions. Their trust in each other justified the decision.

Between the heads of Cosmo and Lorenzo appeared that of Cosmo's elder son, Piero the Gouty. With a combination of ingenuity and tact, Gozzoli placed him so that his lack of a mount – for, in life, his invalidism forced him to travel by litter – was not apparent. The two other members of the family completed the line. At the outside was Cosmo's younger son, Giovanni, his

Opposite: *The Palazzo Medici, designed by Michelozzo, a pupil of Donatello: the ground floor consists of rough-hewn blocks straight from the quarry, the second storey is Doric, the third Corinthian.*

The return of Cosmo de' Medici from his exile.

Fresco by Giorgio Vasari.

55

Piero de' Medici, Lorenzo's father: marble bust by Mino da Fiesole.

father's favourite who fulfilled all the many duties that Piero was by his ill-health unable to do.

Next to him came Lorenzo's only son, the juvenile Pierfrancesco, astride a great white horse, contrasting dramatically with his father's ambling mule beside it. As if to emphasise the difference young Pierfrancesco's horse is adorned with a single diamond. It was almost as if Gozzoli had been gifted with second-sight – unless this particular part of the fresco was not painted till the following year – for in 1440, to Cosmo's great grief, Lorenzo died and

Giovanni de' Medici, Piero's brother: marble bust by Mino da Fiesole.

Pierfrancesco inherited all his wealth which he administered so badly and ostentatiously that a split developed in the family which was never really healed.

It may perhaps be of some assistance to understanding to tabulate the family thus: '1464: Death of Cosmo, leaving his son Piero head of the family. 1469: Death of Piero, leaving his son, Lorenzo the Magnificent head of the family.' But it would be fatal to an appreciation of the realities of the situation if this were taken to mean: 'In 1464 Cosmo died, leaving Piero to move into

the palace and assume the responsibilities of patronage and in 1469 Piero died, leaving his son, Lorenzo the Magnificent, to move into the palace and assume the responsibilities of patronage.'

For the essential factor in Lorenzo the Magnificent's early life and education was that the family all lived under the same roof and had done so for nearly a decade before Lorenzo was born. And that until 1463 – that is to say until Lorenzo was twelve – the dominant figure was Giovanni, his uncle, who, because of Piero's wretched health, was tacitly regarded by everyone as the heir. Also, for the whole period from their occupation of their palazzo in 1440 till Giovanni's death in 1463, the family acted as a unit – Cosmo directing everything with Giovanni as his trusted executive and Piero supervising the collection of books and artistic treasures and selecting artists for contemporary patronage. (Cosmo's own predominant artistic interest was architecture.)

Similarly the women of the household were complementary. Cosmo's wife, Contessina, was the archetypal housewife, preoccupied with the health of the family and the state of their wardrobes, with the making of oil and cheese on the Medici farms in the countryside around and arranging for the transport and care of the bedding on their summer visits to Careggi or Caffagiolo, their villas in the hills. Lucrezia, Piero's wife, was an ideal helpmate in his cultural interests and, in addition to her own writing, was a discriminating patroness – Botticelli was her most famous protégé – and, throughout her life, the dominating influence on her son, Lorenzo the Magnificent, who wrote on the day of her death in 1482 that she was 'my only refuge amid my many cares and difficulties; the only helper who could aid and counsel me'.

The preoccupations of Giovanni's wife, Ginevra, seem to have been mainly social. She gave her husband one son, who died in childhood, two years before his father. On Giovanni's death in 1463, the whole balance of the family was altered and Cosmo, himself in his last illness, had himself carried through all the rooms of his great palace, now completed, repeating again and again: 'Too large a house now for so small a family!'

But in 1440, the future seemed assured. Among the celebrities from the East who attended the council the most important was the seventy-year-old Greek scholar, Gemistos who, out of reverence for Plato, had changed his name to Plethon and made his mission in life the propagation of a version of Platonic philosophy mixed with a curious kind of Oriental mysticism and magic which he called Zoroastrianism. This, by founding 'Platonic academies'

Opposite: *The new church of San Lorenzo, commissioned by the Medici family, and designed by Brunelleschi.*

where circumstances were propitious, he attempted to substitute for the accepted Christian values. He attended the council at Florence as one of the six champions of the Eastern Church to debate against the Roman Church of the West. As he had in fact renounced Christianity in favour of Neo-Platonism, he spent his time discoursing on Platonism and Zoroastrianism to the Florentines and so fascinated Cosmo himself that, shortly afterwards, a Platonic Academy was formed and given hospitality for its meetings in the new palace.

Cosmo had his own reasons, which were not merely aesthetic, for seeking some compromise with Christian beliefs. He talked not only to Plethon but to the Pope. A friend and admirer of Cosmo recorded: 'In the arrangement and administration of affairs of the city, it could not fail that his conscience was loaded with many things, as is usually the case with those who govern states and rule others. He perceived that if he wished to preserve himself in his position and obtain the mercy of God, works of piety were necessary. As it now appeared to him that a part of his possessions, I know not how, had been obtained in a doubtful manner, he wished to roll off this burden from his shoulders, and poured out his heart to Pope Eugenius IV, who was then in Florence, begging him to tell him how he could lighten his conscience.'

An outward and visible sign of efforts to lighten it was obviously the building and renovation of churches and convents, including the church in which Eugenius was particularly interested – the church and convent of San Marco, about quarter of a mile from the Medici palace, which the Pope had just granted to the Dominican Order. Cosmo immediately commissioned Michelozzo to design an elaborate new building which the Dominican friar, Fra Angelico of Fiesole – a man of such holiness that, as has been truly said of him, 'he lived in an unfatigued veracity of eternal light, having in him an ever-flowing river of holy thought, with God for its source, God for its shore and God for its ocean' – decorated with frescoes unmatched in the history of painting. Fra Angelico, with his brother Bennedetto and his best pupil, Benozzo Gozzoli, and other helpers, also painted frescoes in the individual cells of the friars. Cosmo himself had a double cell allotted to him, to which he could retire from time to time as an escape from the business of the world or as a change from the atmosphere of the Platonic Academy where a lamp burned before the bust of Plato.

Opposite: *Some of the treasures belonging to the Medici family.*

Overleaf: *Cosmo de' Medici commissioned Benozzo Gozzoli to paint* The Journey of the Magi *in 1439: this detail represents Lorenzo the Magnificent on horseback in the role of the Third King*

In so far as he could, he tried to reconcile the two opposing worlds by founding and housing in his palace a great library of classical and early Christian literature. It was started in 1440, under Piero's charge, and was the first public library in Europe, for any scholar was allowed to use it. Among its treasures were the original copy of the *Pandects* of Justinian; the best manuscript of Cicero's letters; two manuscripts of Tacitus, one of them being the only known copy containing the first five books of the *Annals*; the only ancient copy of Sophocles's tragedies; a Greek treatise on surgery; a Syriac Gospel of A.D. 556; the Bible copied from 690 to 716 by the Abbot of Wearmouth and known as the *Codex Amiatinus*; early copies of Pliny, Virgil and the *Commentaries* of Julius Caesar and, of 'modern' works, many connected with the great Florentine poets, Petrarch and Dante.

When, a few years later, printing was invented, neither Cosmo nor Piero nor Lorenzo the Magnificent after him eschewed printed books, as many rival collectors did on the ground that they were crude and ugly and eventually the Medici Library came to possess some among its more than ten thousand priceless manuscripts.

In later years, when the glory of the Medici had long departed, there was set in the courtyard of the palace a Latin inscription to remind the visitor where he was: 'Once the house of the Medici (*Mediceas olim aedes*) in which not alone many great men but Knowledge herself had her home. The house which was the nurse of all learning; which here revived again.'

Thus it might be said that the most important factor in the education of Lorenzo the Magnificent was simply that he was born in the Palazzo Medici and grew up in it – that he could help his father in the little study Piero had made for himself on the first floor, his *scrittoio*, where specially constructed wooden cabinets housed the priceless collection of vases and jewels and *objets d' art*; that from his poetess-mother he got encouragement to write little verses in the vernacular and from her passionate Christianity learnt to attend Mass as the first duty of the day and on many evenings to accompany her to meetings of the Fraternity of St Paul where the Christian virtues were expressed in such practical forms as providing dowries for poverty-stricken girls, supporting poor convents and nunneries and apportioning extensive alms for distribution to the destitute; that his uncle Giovanni could instruct him not only on the merits of horses but on the family code of behaviour on state occasions so that, for instance, when the Milanese nobility were entertained at the palace, the visitors were surprised to see that neither Giovanni nor his young nephew sat at table, but busied themselves waiting on the

Opposite: *The Medici family's villa at Careggi, where Lorenzo spent much of his childhood, and where he died.*

guests; and that from his grandfather he learnt the appreciation of nature, helping Cosmo in the vineyard at Careggi or in laying-out a new and beautiful garden for San Marco. And with older sisters to contend with and a younger brother, Giuliano, to care for, Lorenzo experienced the normal strains and stresses of family life.

His formal education, which was started at the age of five under a tutor, Gentile Becchi, was mainly classical and by the time he was ten, his master was able to report to Piero that 'he was well on with Ovid'. Among other accomplishments he was taught to sing to his own accompaniment on the lyre and his other tutor, the young Marsilio Ficino, a Humanist engaged in translating Plato into Latin, reported disapprovingly that the boy 'sang

Opposite: The library in San Marco, the Dominican friary for the building of which Cosmo assumed financial responsibility in 1437.

Below: Cosmo had a double cell allotted to himself in the convent of San Marco, where he could retire from time to time from the business of the world.

spiritual songs as if he were driven by a divine fury'. Always, for Lorenzo, his mother's influence was to overtop any other.

Lucrezia was instrumental in having put on record a picture of the family painted for her husband in the year 1465, when Cosmo had just died and, with Giovanni also dead, the frail Piero had to face the responsibilities of rule. The picture was the work of her protégé, the twenty-year-old Sandro Botticelli, who had already painted a *Judith* to match her long religious poem on the subject, and whom she had first discovered when he was painting frescoes for the Tornabuoni villa. Piero and Lucrezia took this obvious genius into the Palazzo Medici, treated him almost like a son – he was only five years older than Lorenzo – and kept him continuously occupied in painting pictures for which they paid him liberally.

It has been truly said of Botticelli that 'many of his most important pictures cannot be understood at all without a full knowledge of the history of the period'. And certainly those of his first years, after his apprenticeship to Fra Filippo Lippi was over and he had become a member of the Medici household, necessitate a knowledge of his patrons' circumstances, while at the same time his extraordinary sensitivity to atmosphere combined with his devotion to Lucrezia and Piero make him an invaluable interpreter of their thought.

Thus while *The Madonna of the Magnificat* pleases the art-connoisseur because it 'expresses a depth of divine tenderness and a deep spiritual feeling such as no other painter, not even Raphael has reached', to the historian it presents Piero's family as it was at the time of Cosmo's dying sadness for its 'smallness' and the more appropriate name for it is that by which it is only sometimes known *The Madonna of the 'Humilitas'*. The Madonna (Lucrezia) is writing the *Magnificat*, dipping her pen in an ink-pot held by Lorenzo, while Giuliano holds the book in which she writes it. Behind the boys, protectively, stands their eldest sister, Maria, a hand on the shoulder of each. The two other girls, Nannina and Biana, hold a crown above Our Lady's head. The Child – the only grandchild of the family – points to the word *Humilitas* in the manuscript – while his other hand rests on a crushed pomegranate, the 'apple' of Eden, signifying pride. Through the window can be seen the countryside and the villa of Careggi.

It was now time for Lorenzo to take his place as an executive of the small family. When he was sixteen Piero sent him to Milan as his proxy at the wedding of the Duke's son. On the way he was to visit Bologna, Venice and Ferrara to make first-hand investigations of the Medici banks there. 'This

Opposite: *Botticelli's* Madonna del Magnificat *imposed the faces of Piero de' Medici's wife and children on the Holy Family.*

journey is a touchstone of your abilities', said his father. 'Do not care for expense; think only of doing honour to your family. Think of showing that you are now a man and not a boy.' And as soon as he had left, his mother wrote: 'I am lonely, forsaken and sad without you, but I rejoice in your journey in which you will see many remarkable things which will delight your mind.'

So Lorenzo entered the last, the practical, stage of his education – a powerfully built, broad-chested and agile youth, but lacking physical beauty, with a sallow complexion, a flattened nose and a sharp chin. He lacked almost entirely any sense of smell, but, characteristically accounted this a blessing, as he found most smells unpleasant.

Ceramic medallion by Luca della Robbia, with the iris of Florence.

His Father's Helper

Cosmo's most notable piece of statesmanship had been to reverse the foreign policy of Florence. Instead of an alliance with Venice and a perpetual state of war with Milan, he chose to ally himself with the great *condottiore*, Francesco Sforza, who had made himself Duke of Milan, and to incur the hostility of Venice which was less dangerous as an enemy and less valuable as a friend than was Milan.

This change had gradually been accepted and had made Florence under the Medici virtually the arbiter of Italy, but personal jealousies and feuds still persisted and the next mission on which Piero sent Lorenzo tested his diplomatic ability to the utmost. The youth of seventeen had to visit the new Pope, Paul II, who was a Venetian businessman (it was only when his uncle had become Pope Eugenius IV that he decided that the Church might offer a better career) notorious for his avarice. And Lorenzo's task was to get a concession to work the newly discovered alum mines at Tolfa on Papal territory. Alum was essential for the textile industry, as it was used in the dyeing of wool and silk in the most popular colours.

Lorenzo was, of course, aided and advised by his maternal, Tornabuoni, uncles who managed the Rome branch of the Medici bank, but his success in extracting valuable concessions from the Pope was essentially a tribute to his own personality and powers of persuasion; and his father was well enough pleased with him to give him an even more difficult assignment. While he was in Rome, Francesco Sforza, Duke of Milan, died suddenly and it was possible that some of the Italian cities would take advantage of the succession of his weak, incompetent son to stir up trouble. The one most likely to was Ferrante, King of Naples, so to him Lorenzo was now sent to discover how the land lay.

Ferdinand of Naples, more usually referred to as Don Ferrante, was the bastard of a half-caste Moor and a Spanish lady, had been adopted by the great Alfonso of Naples as his son and heir and now, at the age of forty-four,

71

had reigned for ten years, to the misery of his subjects and the apprehension of the rest of Italy. There was, they said, no crueller man in the world. There was no measure against the Neapolitans from which he shrank. By his personal monopoly of corn and oil, he controlled the sources of life for the poor. By forced loans, confiscations and executions, he pillaged the rich. His greatest pleasure, of which he made no secret, was to have his enemies near him, either lingeringly alive in his prisons or dead and embalmed, wearing the clothes they had worn in their lifetime in his museum of mummies. Restless, active, violent by nature, of profound dissimulation and insatiably ambitious there was nothing from which he would shrink in his determination to make himself master of the whole of Italy.

On such a man it was quite impossible for Lorenzo to exert any influence

nor, indeed, did his father expect it. All that Piero was concerned with was a report of Ferrante's intentions. Nevertheless Lorenzo contrived to fascinate the calamitous tyrant sufficiently for an understanding to be formed which, many years later, was to save both Lorenzo and Florence at a crisis of their history.

And quite apart from any immediate practical result, Lorenzo found it invaluable to have had personal meetings with a pope who was an ostentatious, profligate and illiterate businessman and a king who ruled by naked, ruthless power. It increased his respect for his own bourgeois status as a factor in popularity indispensable in Florence.

Lorenzo the Magnificent is received by Don Ferrante on his arrival in Naples: fresco by Vasari.

Pisanello's medal of Francesco Sforza, Duke of Milan, with whom Cosmo de' Medici allied Florence.

Also it gave him a self-assurance which, on his return home, he found that he needed in a situation of menace to the Medici. By the enfeeblement of the family by the deaths of Cosmo and Giovanni, the increasing illness of Piero and Lorenzo's own youth, the enemies and rivals of the Medici considered the time convenient to overthrow them. The leader of the anti-Medici faction was Luca Pitti, an immensely wealthy entrepreneur in raw French cloth who had benefited by Cosmo's largesse – a man greedy, ungrateful and with a mania for *grandezza*. Partly to gratify this, partly to frame his challenge in a way the Florentine would understand, he started to build himself a palace on the south bank of the Arno which was to be larger than the Palazzo Medici and which stood in a kind of royal isolation, very different from the Medici palace in the heart of the city. The rival buildings gave the parties their names – the Mountain, because Pitti's house was on the slope of the hill of San Giorgio, and the Plain, because the Medici's was in the level centre of the city.

The most important associates of Pitti in the Mountain were the Neroni brothers, Giovanni who was Archbishop of Florence and almost as devoted as the Pope himself to the service of Mammon, and Diotsalvi, a banker who had been one of Cosmo's most intimate and trusted advisers and whom he had commended to Piero. Diotsalvi, playing upon Piero's habitual liking for order and neatness, had suggested that his first action on assuming the responsibilities of the headship of the family should be to ascertain its exact financial position by calling in the loans which, often without insistence on

Left: *Pope Paul II's seal, attributed to Giuliano degli Scipioni.* Right: *Anonymous terra-cotta bust of the villainous Luca Pitti, who planned the murder of Piero de' Medici.*

strict repayment from personal friends, the old man had made in those last years when his prime object had been the salvation of his own soul.

Piero ingenuously followed Neroni's advice, with the result that many businesses were ruined for want of credit and many citizens bankrupted. Within eighteen months, Neroni's calculations had succeeded beyond expectation and so many powerful friends of the father had become relentless enemies of the son that the once-powerful party of the Medici was almost at vanishing point. It needed but the slightest push, so the Neroni and Pitti estimated, for it to collapse; and collapse could be made certain by the murder of Piero.

The day chosen for his assassination was St Bartholomew's Eve – August 23, 1466 – on which day it was known that Piero insisted on being taken by litter from Careggi, where he was convalescing from a serious attack of his illness, to the Medici palace, so that he might be in the centre of things in

Florence for the assembly of the New *Signoria* on September 1.

Lorenzo, who had been staying with his father at Careggi since his return from Naples, had left the villa early that morning, leaving Piero to follow at his leisurely pace a little later. As he rode down the accustomed road into the city, past the neighbouring villa of Sant' Antonio, which was the country house of the Archbishop of Florence, Lorenzo became aware of a number of suspicious persons and overheard enquiries as to the whereabouts of his father. He immediately sent back a message to the officer in charge of Piero's litter, bidding him to take a different route into Florence from the one they had agreed upon and habitually used. Thus Piero avoided passing the Archbishop's residence which was filled with hired ruffians placed there by Diotsalvi Neroni with his brother, the Archbishop's, connivance and blessing, to perpetrate the murder.

Once safely in Florence, Piero denounced the Neroni, with Luca Pitti and the other conspirators, to the *Signoria*, with the result that the laymen were officially exiled, while the Archbishop fled precipitately to Rome.

Piero, however, refused to take any measures against Pitti himself. 'The man who does not know how to forgive', he told Lorenzo, 'does not know how to rule', and his generosity to Pitti won him from hostility to devoted friendship. It was the citizens of Florence who punished the conspirator by an unparalleled public ostracism. 'His house', wrote Machiavelli, 'now presented only a vast solitude where previously crowds of citizens had assembled. In the streets his friends and relatives, instead of accompanying him, were afraid even to salute him. Many who had presented to him articles of value now demanded them back as being only lent and those who had been wont to extol him as a man of surpassing excellence now described him as being violent and ungrateful.' Unkindest cut of all, the builders and workmen, who had been devoted to him, refused to have anything to do with him, so that his great palace remained for generations unfinished – and when at last it was it was taken over by the Medici.

Meanwhile the exiled conspirators determined on war with Florence and approached the great Venetian *condottiere* Bartolomeo Colleone, who at seventy-five was still seeking new worlds to conquer and wished to spend his last years as one of the Italian princes in the way that his peer among the captains of mercenaries, Francesco Sforza, had made himself Duke of Milan. Colleone gladly assented and made preparations to attack Florence from the

Opposite: *Federigo da Montefeltro, Duke of Urbino, by Piero della Francesca.*

Overleaf: *Botticelli's* The Adoration of the Magi, *in which four generations of the Medici are portrayed.*

Romagna, whose petty lords welcomed war which made it possible for them to get more from the sale of their swords than from the tenants who cultivated their lands.

To counter Colleone, Piero renewed the Triple Alliance of Florence, Naples and Milan as 'The League for the Peace of Italy' and welcomed to Florence Ferrante's son, Federigo, with a Neapolitan force and the young Duke, Galeazzo Sforza, at the head of one from Milan, to give reality to it.

He also ordered Sandro Botticelli to paint a picture *The Adoration of the Magi*, as a votive offering to be placed in Santa Maria Novella in thanksgiving for the deliverance of himself and his family from the danger of the Pitti conspiracy. Here the artist excelled himself in giving portraits of the elder branch of the Medici, in a design where the symmetry stresses their relationship roughly in the form of a genealogical tree. The top-most face, far above the others, that of St Joseph, is Giovanni 'Bicci', the founder; beneath him his son, Cosmo, *Pater Patriae*, as the first King; beneath Cosmo in an arc are the heads of his three sons, recognisably brothers, in the order of their ages – his illegitimate son, Carlo (the only one of them wearing a hat), who was at the time an Apostolic Notary and Governor of Prato; Piero kneeling, in the centre, as the second King; and to his right, the beloved Giovanni; then, standing, at the bottom corners of the picture, Lorenzo and Giuliano, represented the fourth generation.

Lorenzo is given a large sword, which he holds before him with both hands, to indicate the signification of the picture – an allusion to the fact that by his courage and sagacity he had been the saviour of his father's life and indirectly, of the whole family from ruin. And, as if to emphasise the point, Botticelli makes Lorenzo's gaze fixed steadily on his father, oblivious of the conversation of his companions.

As the picture was a *pièce d'occasion* and managed so admirably to fulfil its particular purpose, the artist may be forgiven the uncharacteristic representation of Lorenzo with a sword. For the one thing Lorenzo was not was a soldier. Though he had a passion for horses and hunting and a penchant for tournaments, he had neither taste for nor knowledge of the art of war. The general conduct of 'the Colleonic War', as it came to be called, was entrusted to Federigo da Montefeltro, Duke of Urbino, whose military reputation equalled that of Colleone himself and whose pretensions as a connoisseur made him exclude printed books from his impressive library. To Lorenzo fell the duty of representing Piero as head of the State – 'without

Opposite: *The courtyard of the Bargello, administrative centre of Florence.*

him I am like a man without hands', his father proclaimed – of organising the finances of the campaign and of reconciling the citizens as well as he could to the heavy taxation it involved.

In spite of a Florentine victory at Molinella the one pitched battle that the opposing sides could bring themselves to fight (at the conclusion of which the rival *condottieri* ritually embraced each other in mutual congratulation at their personal survival), the war dragged on until the April of 1468 when it became clear that it was to no one's advantage to continue it and Colleone was despatched by Venice, at an astronomical salary, against the Turks.

Piero celebrated the conclusion of hostilities in his accustomed private fashion by commissioning a picture from Botticelli. The Council of the Mercantanzia had just arranged for Piero Pollajuolo to decorate the backs of the new seats of the judges with representations of the virtues Prudence, Charity, Temperance, Fortitude, Justice and Faith. Piero requested that one of these, the fourth, should be executed by Botticelli. The request was, of course, granted. The cold courage of endurance, which is Fortitude, was something Piero understood and his associates honoured him for.

Ruskin, in his memorable description of the picture, has conveyed unwittingly (for he was uninterested in, if not quite ignorant of, the historical circumstances of its painting) how the artist made it a memorial to his beloved patron: 'I promised some note of Sandro's *Fortitude*. I've lost my own notes and cannot now remember whether she has a sword or a mace – it does not matter. What is chiefly notable in her is that you would not, if you had to guess who she was, take her for Fortitude at all. Everybody else's Fortitude announce themselves clearly and proudly. They have tower-like shields and lion-like helmets, and stand firm astride on their legs and are confidently ready for all comers.

'But Botticelli's Fortitude is no match, it may be, for any that are coming. Worn, somewhat, and not a little weary, instead of standing ready for all comers, she is sitting, apparently in reverie, her fingers playing restlessly and idly – nay, I think, even nervously – about the hilt of her sword. For her battle is not to begin today; nor did it begin yesterday. Many a morn and eve have passed since it began; and now – is this to be the ending day of it? And if this – by what manner of end?

'That is what Sandro's Fortitude is thinking and the playing fingers about the sword-hilt would fain let it fall, if it might be; and yet, how swiftly and gladly will they close on it when the far-off trumpet blows, which she will hear through all her reverie.'

Opposite: *Botticelli's* Fortitude.

By the summer of 1468 it was clear that Piero had little time left and that there was one last thing he must attend to. A wife must be found for Lorenzo.

The wife eventually chosen for Lorenzo was Clarice, the sixteen-year-old daughter of a Roman nobleman of the powerful Orsini family famed for its military prowess and its political pretensions. Piero shrewdly abandoned the Medici custom of making marriage alliances with other Florentine families which (inevitably in the claustrophobic atmosphere of jealous rivalries and feuds) resulted in making as many enemies as friends. And in choosing a famous fighting clan with large estates both to the north and south of Rome, he hoped to do something to rectify Florence's military weakness. He was, of course, unable himself to travel to Rome, but the marriage negotiations were in the capable hands of his wife and her brothers.

Lucrezia's letters to her husband from Rome were as accomplished as became an authoress. Describing her first meeting with Clarice and her mother, she wrote: 'Madonna Maddalena Orsini entered with her daughter, who wore a closely-fitting dress, such as the Roman women wear, and was without a kerchief on her head. Our conversation lasted for some time, so that I had an opportunity of looking at her. The girl is above the middle height, of fair complexion and pleasant manners, and, if less beautiful than our daughters, of great modesty; so that it will be easy to teach her our manners. She is not blonde, for no one is so here and her thick hair has a reddish tinge. Her face is round, but does not displease me. Her neck is beautiful, but rather thin – or, rather, delicately shaped. Her breasts I could not see, as here they cover them entirely, but they seemed to me well-formed. She does not hold her head as proudly as our girls do but inclines it a little forward, which I take to be due to the timidity which is the predominant feature of her character. Her hands are long and delicate. On the whole, the girl seems to be of the ordinary type but she is not to be compared with our Maria, Lucrezia [Nannina] and Bianca. Lorenzo has seen her himself and he will tell you whether she pleases him. I am sure that whatever you and he decide will be good. May God rule it for the best!'

(Lorenzo had presumably seen his bride-to-be during his visit to Rome, but it is doubtful whether he had taken any particular notice of her and to the highest degree unlikely that his wishes were consulted in the matter. When the marriage eventually took place, he was careful to note in his diary: 'I took to wife Clarice, the daughter of the Lord Jacopo Orsini – or, rather, she was given to me.')

Opposite: *Bartolomeo Colleoni, after whom the 'Colleonic War' was named, was so ambitious that he was easily incited to lead the forces of Pitti and Neroni against Florence : detail from the monument sculpted by Verrocchio.*

'The girl's father', Lucrezia's letter continued, 'is Signor Jacopo Orsini of Monterotondo, her mother Cardinal Orsini's sister. She has two brothers; one has devoted himself to arms and stands in good repute with the Lord Orso; the other is priest and Papal sub-deacon. They possess half of Monterotondo; the other half belongs to their uncle, who has two sons and three daughters. Besides this, three castles belong to them – that is to say, to the brothers of the girl and, from what I hear, they are rich and likely to become richer. For, not to mention that they are on their mother's side the nephews of the Cardinal-Archbishop and the knight, they are on their father's side cousins in the second degree to these lords who have great affection for them. This is about all that I have learned. I think of leaving on Monday week and will write to you on the way. I am not writing to Madonna Contessina as it seems unnecessary. Commend me to her and greet the girls and Lorenzo and Giuliano. Your Lucrezia. Rome, March 28, 1467.'

For the rest of the year and the greater part of 1468, the two families bargained over the marriage settlement, with the respective uncles of the bride and bridegroom – the Cardinal and the banker Giovanni Tornabuoni – playing the leading parts. On November 27, 1468 the Cardinal was able to write to Piero: 'Thank God it is concluded to the welfare of your house and ours, for it is a joy to us old people as well as to the women and the young folks. Illustrious Piero, I esteem the new relationship very highly. You do not need the possessions of others and yours remain to you.'

The marriage was celebrated by proxy in Rome with Filippo de' Medici, Archbishop of Pisa, a distant relative, representing the bridegroom. After the ceremony he wrote to Lorenzo: 'I have today espoused the noble and illustrious Madonna Clarice degli Orsini in your name; in my opinion a maiden of such physical gifts, appearance and manners deserves no other bridegroom than him whom, I believe, Heaven has destined for her. You must thank God for the protection He has afforded you in this matter, as in other things depending on good luck.'

Lorenzo, however, showed no disposition to make the journey to Rome to see his wife and bring her to Florence and she was still living with her parents when she wrote to him on February 25, 1469: 'Illustrious consort, I have received a letter from you which has given me great pleasure, wherein you inform me of the tournament at which you won the prize. I am glad you are successful in what gives you pleasure and that my prayer is heard, as I have no other wish than to see you happy.'

The tournament, known simply as 'Lorenzo's Tournament', had taken place on February 7 as the official celebration of his marriage. His own account

Opposite: *Courtyard in the Medici Palace.*

86

of it ran: 'I held a joust on the Piazza of Santa Croce, at great expense and with much pomp, on which I find about 10,000 ducats were spent. Although neither my years nor my blows were very great, the first prize was awarded to me, a silver helmet with Mars as its crest.'

In contrast to this factual simplicity, the lengthy poem by Luigi Pulci, *La Giostra di Lorenzo de' Medici*, described in painstaking detail the most splendid joust Florence had ever seen. The lists were prepared with great magnificence in the piazza of Santa Croce. There were eighteen competitors and among the judges sat the noted *condottiere* Roberto da Sanseverino. The approach of Lorenzo's procession was hailed by the crowd with frantic applause. First came nine trumpeters and three pages of whom one carried Lorenzo's personal standard of silver and crimson. They were flanked by two squires in full armour whom the Duke of Urbino (Piero's bibliophilic rival) and Sanseverino had placed at Lorenzo's disposal. Then came twelve nobles on horseback accompanying Lorenzo's brother, the fifteen-year-old Giuliano dressed in a tabard of silk brocade, a doublet embroidered with pearls and silver and a black velvet cap adorned with three feathers made of gold thread and set with large pearls and rubies.

Five mounted pages and a line of drummers and fifers now led the way for Lorenzo himself. He was mounted on a great white horse, richly caparisoned in red and white velvet, adorned with pearls – the gift of Ferrante of Naples. He wore a surcoat with a shoulder-piece of red and white silk and across it a silk scarf embroidered with fresh and withered roses with the motto *Le Temps Revient* picked out in pearls. On his velvet cap was a feather worked in gold thread, set with rubies and diamonds and having in the centre a pearl worth five hundred gold florins. The centre-piece of his shield was the treasured Medici diamond, 'Il Libro', valued at two thousand florins and the device on the shield, gold fleur-de-lys on an azure ground, announced to the spectators what was at the moment the proudest boast of the family – that Louis XI had recently granted to Piero and his heirs, as a token of his admiration, the right to wear the royal arms of France in perpetuity. Ten horsemen and sixty-four footmen armed and helmeted completed Lorenzo's retinue.

For the tournament itself, he changed his velvet surcoat for one also bearing the French arms and donned a helmet surmounted by the three feathers which Cosmo long ago had adopted as the private Medici crest, signifying the virtues of truth, prudence and fortitude. Lorenzo also changed

Opposite: *A page from an early edition of* La Giostra di Lorenzo de Medici *in which the author Luigi Pulci describes the tournament held to celebrate Lorenzo's marriage.*

CLA GIOSTRA DI LORENZO
DE MEDICI MESSA IN RI
MA DA LVIGI DE PVL
CI ANNO . M . CCCC
LXVIII.

SIO MERITAI DI TE MIO
SACro Apollo
Quel di chio uenni altuo
famoso templo
Et piansi tanto del suo extremo crollo
Accioche a tuoi suggecti ancho sia exemplo
Io son soletto apie dun erto collo
Aiuta el suono che per piacerti tempro
Ad cantar uersi del tuo amato lauro
Se tiricorda gia de bei crin dauro

Se tiricorda anchor del tempo antico
Se ilbel Hiacynto o Climen mai tipiacque
Dapoi che del tuo amor qui canto & dico
Onde ilprincipio della giostra nacque

Inuocati-
one.

a i

his horse for one which had been sent him by the Marquis of Este.

His first joust was with Carlo Borromeo; the second with Braccio de' Medici, a distant cousin, who attacked him with such ferocity that – according to the poet-reporter – 'if the stroke had taken place Orlando himself could not have survived the shock'. Lorenzo returned the attack with equal vehemence but his lance splintered and his adversary was saved from total overthrow. His third opponent was Carlo da Forme, whose helmet he split and whom he nearly unhorsed.

Lorenzo then changed his horse for one which had been given him by the Duke of Milan and prepared to face Benedetto Salutati who had just couched his lance. Of this bout Pulci wrote:

> Hast thou not seen the falcon in his flight,
>> When high in air on balanced wing he hung
> On some lone straggler of the covey light?
>> On Benedetto thus Lorenzo sprung.
> Whistled the air, as ardent for the fight,
>> Fleet as the arrow flies he rushed along.
>>> Achilles's rage their meeting strokes inspires;
>>> Their sparkling armour rivals Etna's fires!

Lorenzo was equally successful in the remaining bouts, including that with his brother-in-law, Gugliemo de' Pazzi, Bianca's husband, and at the close of the tournament was adjudged the victor and escorted ceremonially from the lists wearing the silver helmet, surmounted by the figure of Mars, which was the prize.

At whose hands he received it is not known though his biographers, following contemporary gossips in constructing what they consider an appropriate love-life for their hero, assume it was Lucrezia Donati whom he had first met earlier when he was sixteen and she eleven. Some go so far as to assert that the tournament was given in her honour – which, in the circumstances, seems an improbable discourtesy. If it was not to celebrate his marriage, it was more likely to have been given for the reason asserted by the historian of Florence, Niccolo Machiavelli – to distract the attentions of the citizens from the tense political situation inseparable from the uncertainties attendant on the slow dying of Piero.

The general air of Florentine festivity and Medici greatness was continued in preparations for the reception of Clarice Orsini, who left Rome on May 15, 1469 to be married in person on Sunday, June 4. All the towns and villages

Opposite: *Verrocchio's bust of an unknown woman is thought to represent Lucrezia Donati.*

in Florentine territory sent their presents – food and sweetmeats, wine and wax, one hundred and fifty calves and more than two thousand pairs of capons and hens which helped to provide for a feast given to eight hundred citizens.

On the appointed day, Clarice who had been lodged in the Albizzi quarter of the city, made a state entrance into the Medici palace, which had been temporarily enlarged for the occasion by a great ballroom built out into the Via Larga, and on her arrival, dressed in white and gold and riding Ferrante's gift horse, an olive-tree was drawn up to the upper windows by a contrivance similar to that used at the annual feast of St John the Baptist. After the wedding-ceremony in the tiny chapel of the house, the banquet of over fifty dishes (and sweetmeats estimated at over five thousand pounds) was provided for about two thousand guests. The bride and about fifty young married women dined in the loggia of the garden; in the colonnades enclosing the courtyard on three sides about seventy of the most distinguished men; in the hall of the ground floor about thirty-six young people; and in the hall of the first floor about forty older ladies with Madonna Lucrezia presiding. The number of courses was not great 'in order to give the citizens an example of moderation which must not be forgotten at weddings'.

The festivities continued until the Tuesday when they all went to Mass in San Lorenzo and Clarice was presented with a Book of Hours 'of wonderful beauty', golden letters on a blue ground with a binding of silver and crystal which was said to have cost the donor two hundred florins.

Thus was Lorenzo de' Medici married to Clarice degli Orsini, a girl totally uninterested in politics or learning or art, so that to the absence of love was added a notable lack of sympathy with his dominant passions. But this may not have been such a drawback as it appeared, since Lorenzo had already written: 'The defect which is so common in women and which makes them insupportable is their affectation of understanding everything.' And she bore him ten children.

Poet and Lover

Shortly before the tournament, Lorenzo had sent to Ferrante of Naples a book and a letter. Referring to their last meeting, the young man wrote: 'You will remember how you turned the conversation to those who have written poetry in the Tuscan language and showed a desire to see all their works collected by my care. Endeavouring to fulfil your wishes I have had a diligent search made for all the old manuscripts and chosen from them the least imperfect, which I now present to Your Highness, arranged in order in a book, which I hope you will accept as a token of my especial goodwill. No one should despise this Tuscan tongue as poor and rude, for he who can rightly estimate its value will find it rich and cultivated. In fact, there is nothing vigorous or graceful or impressive or ingenious or witty or harmonious or majestic of which examples may not be found in our two greatest poets, Dante and Petrarch.'

After a short discussion of some of their predecessors, including Guinicello 'whom Dante called "his father"' and Calvacanti whose writings Lorenzo found 'in the highest degree attractive' – and a tribute to 'the two glorious suns that have illuminated our language', Dante and Petrarch, Lorenzo introduced some of the best contemporary writers and concluded: 'At the end of the book, as it seemed not unpleasing to you, I have added some sonnets and canzoni of my own so that when you read them my goodwill and affection may be vividly recalled to your mind. Though in themselves unworthy of a place beside the admirable works of the past, it may be useful to set them side by side for a comparison which can but enhance the perfections of the latter. Pray take, O Prince, not only into your house but into your heart and soul, even as you abide a welcome guest in my heart and soul.'

Lorenzo, in time, was to obtain a place in Italian poetry only a little below that of the two 'great suns' and, from his earliest years, poetry was his passion. The order 'poet and lover', at the head of this chapter, is deliberate. As one of his biographers has expressed it: 'In the usual order of things, it is love that

An illustration from a contemporary edition of Stanze, *a book of poems by Angelo Poliziano.*

creates the poet; but with Lorenzo poetry appears to have been the occasion of his love.' This judgment is justified by Lorenzo's own account of matters, which is of cardinal importance to the understanding of his temperament. He wrote autobiographically: 'A young lady of great personal attractions happened to die in Florence; and as she had been very generally admired and loved, so her death was as generally lamented. Almost any person who had any acquaintance with her flattered himself that he had obtained the chief place in her affections. This fatal event excited the extreme sorrow of her admirers; and as she was carried to the place of burial, with her face uncovered, those who had known her when living pressed for a last look at the object of their adoration and accompanied her funeral with their tears "while Death smiled lovely in her lovely face" [Petrarch]. On this occasion all the eloquence and the wit of Florence were exerted in paying due honours to her memory, both in prose and in verse. Among the rest, I also composed a few sonnets; and, in order to give them greater effect I tried to convince myself that I too had been deprived of the object of my love and to excite in my own

Left: *Ghirlandaio's portrait of Luigi Pulci.* Right: *Rosselli's portrait of Angelo Poliziano.*

mind all those passions that might enable me to move the affections of others. Under the influence of this imagination I began to think how sad was the fate of those by whom she had been beloved; and from thence I was led to speculate whether there was any other woman in Florence deserving such honour and praise, and to imagine the happiness that must be experienced by anyone whose good fortune could procure him such a subject for his pen. I accordingly sought for some time without having the satisfaction of finding anyone who, in my judgment, deserved a sincere and constant attachment.'

Lorenzo's self-revelatory admission, can only be appreciated by remembering that, from his earliest years, he was soaked in Platonic philosophy and regarded Platonism as the key to the best way of life. He is not saying, as it might seem to a generation whose thought has been clouded from its cradle by a distorted and bowdlerised idea of Platonic love: 'I am unlikely to find *any* woman worthy of me.' He is saying: 'I am unlikely to find any *woman* to inspire my art.'

Plato's teaching is unequivocal: 'Since Venus is of two natures, Love also must be dual. The elder and motherless goddess is the daughter of Heaven and we call her the Heavenly Venus; and the younger is the daughter of Jove and Dione and we call her the Venus of the People. Necessarily, then, the companion love of the one must be fitly called Popular, and that of the other, Heavenly . . . Now the Love associated with the Venus of the People is of a common nature and functions promiscuously. This love is worshipped by the lower types of men who not only love women and youths equally, but love their bodies more than their souls and prefer the least intelligent among them. For they care only to satisfy their desires and are indifferent whether the manner of their satisfaction be foul or fair. For this love proceeds from the goddess who is not only younger than the other, but has a nature composed of feminine as well as masculine elements. But the other Love is of the Heavenly Venus and is felt only for males. She is the elder also and lust has no part in her; therefore those who are inspired by this love turn to men and love the stronger by nature and the superior by intelligence.'

There were, however, two recent cases in which women were allowed within the masculine province of Platonic love – women who had inspired great poets with whom they had no physical tie – Dante's Beatrice and Petrarch's Laura. It was for a third that Lorenzo was searching.

His account of the quest continues: 'When I had almost abandoned all expectation of success chance threw in my way what had been denied to my most diligent enquiry. A public festival was held in Florence to which I was brought by some of my companions (I suppose as my destiny determined) against my will for I had for some time past avoided such exhibitions or if at times I attended them, it was rather from compliance with custom than for personal pleasure. Among the ladies there assembled I saw one of such sweet and attractive manners that I could not help saying to myself, "If only this person were possessed of the delicacy, the understanding and the accomplishments of her who is lately dead!" '

From the fair unknown (unknown, that is to say, to posterity, for Lorenzo never revealed or even gave a hint of her identity) he asked for a bunch of violets she was holding. On the bunch of violets he managed to write a good sonnet, playing with the conceit that the fresh purple violets took on a richer hue when her white hand has plucked them, just as the touch of her feet in the meadows left the daisies rosy.

Lorenzo described her charms. 'She was of a just and proper height. Her complexion was extremely fair, but not pale; blooming but not ruddy.

Opposite: *In Botticelli's* Birth of Venus *the holder of Venus's cloak was said to represent the beautiful girl whose death all Florence had mourned.*

Her countenance was serious without being severe, mild and pleasant, without levity or vulgarity. Her eyes were lively but without any indication of pride or conceit. Her figure was so finely proportioned that among other women she appeared of superior dignity yet without the least degree of affectation. In walking, in dancing and in other exercises that display the person, every motion was elegant and appropriate.'

As the conventional catalogue continues, the impression grows that the *inamorata* is nothing but the figment of Lorenzo's fancy designed to hang specific poems on and that the real reason for the universal ignorance of her identity is, quite simply, her non-existence. At the same time, the situation conformed admirably to the popularly required pattern and had the double utility of providing one avenue of Florentine gossip while closing – or at least diverting attention from – another.

In Lorenzo's household at the moment were two poets. The elder was Luigi Pulci, who had written the poem on the tournament and whose devotion to Lorenzo shines vividly through his letters, 'Do you really mean to leave me comfortless among these woods while you go to Rome? How often have we talked about Rome and now I shall not be at your side! It would hurt me more than anything else in the world. Do not treat me as if I were old iron, for I shall soon be well if you care for me.' . . . 'If you do not wish people to know that I am your friend, put placards on the walls. Wherever I show myself people whisper "There goes Lorenzo's great friend." ' . . . 'I must have come into the world like hares and other poor animals, doomed to be the prey of the huntsman. It is my fate to love you and be very little in your company.'

The younger poet was Angelo Poliziano, a poor country boy who, at the age of ten, had come to Florence in search of learning and, by the time he was thirteen, had started on a translation of Homer's *Iliad* from Greek into Latin. At fifteen – the year before Lorenzo's tournament – he was already an accomplished poet, and Lorenzo took him into his household and the two remained virtually inseparable till Lorenzo's death. Angelo Poliziano's most remarkable poetic achievement at this time, both for its grace and simplicity and for its blending of joy and sorrow in the evocation of love, was an elegy on a bunch of violets given him by a beloved hand.

In his maturity Poliziano was to become one of the major poets of Italy. 'He and only he', writes John Addington Symonds, 'was destined by combining the finish of the classics with the freshness of a language still in use to inaugurate the golden age of form.' And another critic has pointed out that in

Previous page and opposite: *Details from a painting of a wedding festival by Maestro del Cassone Adimari.*

Lorenzo's two eldest sons: left *Giovanni,* right *Pietro: part of a fresco by Domenico Ghirlandaio.*

Poliziano's poetry 'we have Lorenzo's themes lit up with the warmth and magic radiance of genuine inspiration and in the fancied realms of Poliziano's imagination there is that which is lacking in Lorenzo's.' Whether Lorenzo or Poliziano was the greater poet is largely a matter of personal taste and is, in any event, of no particular interest to any but the devotee of mediaeval Italian poetry. What is important is their personal relationship. It led, not unsurprisingly, to a violent quarrel with Clarice. In due course, Lorenzo appointed 'his Angel' tutor to his children and Poliziano was able to assure him, 'I feel for Piero and your other children an affection equal to that of a father. Should anything unpleasant occur I will endeavour myself to bear it, out of love for you.' It was, of course, impossible for Clarice to accept with equanimity a situation which he thus described to Lorenzo: 'The children are particularly happy. Piero never leaves my side' and he had to admit in a later note: 'We get on as well as we can but I cannot escape a few collisions.'

The final collision came when Lorenzo sent the family into the mountains to escape contact with the plague in Florence. Everything conspired to increase the tensions. Poliziano informed Lucrezia, Lorenzo's mother (with whom, in spite of – or possibly because of – the enmity of Lorenzo's wife, he remained always on excellent terms,) 'The news from this place is that it remains violently and incessantly raining so that it is impossible to leave the house. I do, see, hear nothing that cheers me. In town there is at least some comfort, if it is only that of seeing Lorenzo. Here I have no one to share my thoughts of him and am dying of boredom. And I have not my Madonna Lucrezia to whom I can give vent to my feelings.'

He was released from his boredom by Clarice turning him out. The occasion of the final 'collision' was her insistence that he should use a Psalter, instead of his own classical beginner's book, to start teaching Latin to the three-year-old Giovanni, her second son (who eventually became Pope Leo X).

Poliziano went to the villa of Careggi when he wrote to Lorenzo, 'For decency's sake and not to go to Florence without your orders I came here and am waiting till you inform me what to do; for I am yours though the world itself should turn upside down.'

Lorenzo's reply was to send him to his own private villa at Fiesole, which drew an irritated letter from Clarice: 'It is my wish that Messer Angelo shall not be able to boast of remaining in the household in defiance of me or of your having offered him a home at Fiesole.' Lorenzo's answer was to express his annoyance that Clarice had not sent Poliziano's books to Fiesole and to order that they should all be sent immediately that evening without fail.

It should not be necessary to argue further that the experience of love which Lorenzo sought in order to give depth to his poetry he found in the poet whose name is inseparable from his in the history of that art. 'Poliziano and Lorenzo' are almost a hyphenated word in the story of the Italian Renaissance as representing the first phase of it. Together they broke down the division between popular literature and humanistic culture and gave classic form, hitherto appropriated by scholars, to the poetry and prose of the Italian language, so that henceforward no one would have to apologise for writing in the vulgar tongue. They were both moulders and representatives of the beginning of the true Renaissance – 'serene, self-satisfied, triumphant art, glorying in the beauty of form for form's sake and aiming at perfection in style of sunny and delightful loveliness', in Symonds's words.

Once their personal relationship is taken into account, it becomes much easier to estimate Lorenzo's poetry. Much of it consists of verses made on the same themes as those of Poliziano, as it were in a private competition between them.

Here, for example, is Lorenzo's poem on roses:

> Into a little close of mine I went
>> One morning when the sun with his fresh light
> Was rising all refulgent and unshent.
> Rose-trees are planted there in order bright,
>> Whereto I turned charmed eyes, and long did stay
>> Taking my fill of that new-found delight.
> Red and white roses bloomed upon the spray;
>> One opened leaf by leaf to greet the morn
> Shyly at first, then in sweet disarray;
>> Another, yet a youngling newly born,
>> Scarce struggled from the bud; and there were some
>> Whose petals closed them from the air forlorn;
>> Another fell and showered the grass with bloom.
> Thus I beheld the roses dawn and die
>> And one short hour their loveliness consume.
> But while I watched those languid petals lie
>> Colourless on cold earth, I could but think
>> How vain a thing is youthful bravery.
> Trees have their time to bloom on winter's brink
> Then the rathe blossoms wither in an hour,
>> When the brief days of spring toward summer sink;
> The fruit, as yet unformed, is tart and sour;
> Little by little it grows large and weighs
>> The strong boughs down with slow persistent power;
> Nor without peril can the branches raise
>> Their burden; now they stagger neath the weight
>> Still growing, and are bent above the ways.
> Soon autumn comes and the ripe, ruddy freight
>> Is gathered: the glad season will not stay;
>> Flowers, fruit and leaves are now all desolate.
> Pluck the rose, therefore, maiden, while 'tis May!

Poliziano chose to treat the subject not in the *terza rima* made famous by Dante but in a musical *ballata*, a dance-song:

> I went a-roaming, maidens, one bright day
> In a green garden in mid month of May.

Violets and lilies grew on every side
   Mid the green grass and young flowers wonderful,
Golden and white and red and azure-eyed;
   Towards which I stretched my hands, eager to pull
   Plenty to make my fair curls beautiful
And crown my rippling curls with garlands gay.

I went a-roaming, maidens, one bright day,
In a green garden in mid month of May.

But when my lap was full of flowers I spied
   Roses at last, roses of every hue;
Therefore I ran to pluck their ruddy pride,
   Because their perfume was so sweet and true
   That all my soul went forth with pleasure new,
With yearning and desire too soft to say.

The Medici family's villa at Fiesole, outside Florence, where Lorenzo housed his friend Poliziano, much to Clarice's irritation.

I went a-roaming, maidens, one bright day
In a green garden in mid month of May.

I gazed and gazed. Hard task it were to tell
   How lovely were the roses in that hour;
One was but peeping from her verdant shell,
   And some were faded, others scarce in flower.
Then Love said: 'Go, pluck from the blooming bower
Those that thou seest ripe upon the spray.'

I went a-roaming, maidens, one bright day
In a green garden in mid month of May.

For when the full rose quits her tender sheath,
   When she is sweetest and most fair to see,
Then is the time to place her in thy wreath,
   Before her beauty and her freshness flee.
   Gather ye, therefore, roses with great glee,
Sweet girls, or ere their perfume pass away.

I went a-roaming, maidens, one bright day
In a green meadow in mid month of May.

On this Symonds comments: 'It might almost seem as though Poliziano had rewritten Lorenzo's exercise with a view to showing the difference between true poetry and what is only very like it.'

Lorenzo's early poems are predominantly sonnets, of all poetic forms the most difficult to manage. The dearth of great poetry in sonnet form compared with the plethora of sonnets which are only experiments in versification provoked Dr Johnson's dictum that sonnets are to poetry what carving heads in cherry-stones is to art, but to Lorenzo they may be seen as an attempt to discipline his amazing facility of expression which made it possible for him, for instance, after a long philosophic discussion to turn it into verse as the best method of remembering it and impressing it on his mind.

Lorenzo himself, in the *Commentary* on his poems, argues that the very difficulty of writing a sonnet entitles it to consideration as an art-form superior to most. Its brevity demands that only the right words shall be used and the difficulty of matching thought and expression is increased by the use of rhyme. Of all forms of vernacular poetry the sonnet is the most difficult to bring to perfection and on this account alone it should be esteemed above all

Opposite: *Drawing of a pastoral scene from an early sixteenth-century manuscript of poetry by Lorenzo the Magnificent, Angelo Poliziano, Biagi Buonaccorsi and others.*

Donna uana e il pensiero che mai no crede
Che uenga il tempo della sua uecheza
Et la giouaneza
Habbi sempre ad star ferma i una tempra

Vola iltate et fugge
Presto di ma uita manca el fiore
Et pero de pensare il gentil core
Che ogni cosa reporta iltepo et strugge

Dunq dei gentil donna hauer merzede
Et non di tua belleza ... altera
Pero folle e chi spera
Viuere ingiouaneza et bella sempre

33

LAURENTII MEDICES

E un monte in thessalia detto Pindo
Piu celebrato assai dal sacri uati
Che alcun che sie dal uechio Athlate all indo
A la radice lerbe et fior ben nati
Bagnan lacque dun fote chiare et uiue
Rigando allor fioretti et uerdi prati

Illustration entitled Fontana *from a contemporary edition of* Stanze, *a book of Poetry by Angelo Poliziano.*

others. 'But from this', he adds, 'it must not be inferred that I think that my sonnets have attained to that perfection that properly pertains to this form of verse. For me, it is enough to have made an attempt and if I have not succeeded in driving the chariot of the sun, let it be to me in place of praise that I have been ardent in my endeavours even though my strength has been insufficient for so great an enterprise.'

The dominant theme which emerges from the sonnets is the writer's love of the countryside. He has, indeed, been called the originator of 'Nature Poetry'. 'The central emotion of Lorenzo's verse', wrote Symonds in 1881, 'is scarcely love but delight in the country – the Florentine's enjoyment of the villa, with its woods and rivulets, the pines upon the hillsides, the song-birds and the pleasures of the chase.' As 'a sonnet which might be chosen as a fair specimen of the new manner introduced into literature by Lorenzo' Symonds chooses the following invocation of Venus:

Leave thy belovèd isle, thou Cyprian Queen;
Leave thine enchanted realm so delicate,

Illustration entitled Oratione di Iulio a Pallade *from a contemporary of* Stanze,
a book of poetry by Angelo Poliziano.

Goddess of love! Come where the rivulet
Bathes the short turf and blades of tenderest green!

Come to these shades, these airs that stir the screen
   Of whispering branches and their murmurs set
   To Philomel's enamoured canonzet:
Choose this for thine own land, thy loved demesne!

And if thou com'st by these clear rills to reign,
   Bring thy dear son, thy darling son, with thee,
   For there be none that own his empire here.

From Dian steal the vestals of her train,
   Who roam the woods at will, from danger free,
   And know not love nor his dread anger fear.

In another of the sonnets Lorenzo expatiates on his preference, in place of
the pomp of power and circumstance, for

Un verde praticel pien di bei fiori,
Un rivolo, che l'herba intorno bagni
Un angeletto, che d'Amor si lagni

which has been translated as:

A meadow green of beauteous flowers full,
A streamlet, which the herbage bathes around,
An angel form all languishing with love.

Poliziano was, indeed, conveniently named for poetic purposes. In poem after poem, Lorenzo plays with 'Angelo' in some form or other and Cupid himself becomes an angel:

Ma chi è quel che vola?
È l'Angiolei d'Amore!

But who is this in wingéd flight?
The Angel Bird, the God of Love.

Poliziano, on his side, was able to give more direct acknowledgment of his love.

High-born Lorenzo! Laurel, in whose shade
  Thy Florence rests, nor fears the lowering storm,
Nor threatening signs in Heaven's high front displayed,
  Nor Jove's dread anger in its fiercest form;
O to the trembling muse afford thine aid!
  The muse that courts thee, timorous and forlorn,
    Lives in the shadow of thy prosperous tree
    And binds her every fond desire to thee.

Ere long the spirit that this frame inspires
  – This frame that from its earliest hour was thine –
If Fortune frowns not on my vast desires
  Shall spread to distant shores thy name divine.

Nor did he cease till, shortly after Lorenzo's death, he died of a broken heart, singing to his last his unfinished *Monody* for his lover:

Who from perennial streams shall bring
Of gushing floods a ceaseless spring?
That through the day, in hopeless woe
And through the night my tears may flow.

Opposite: *Manuscript of Poliziano's* Monody *on the death of Lorenzo, set to music by Arrigo Isaac.*

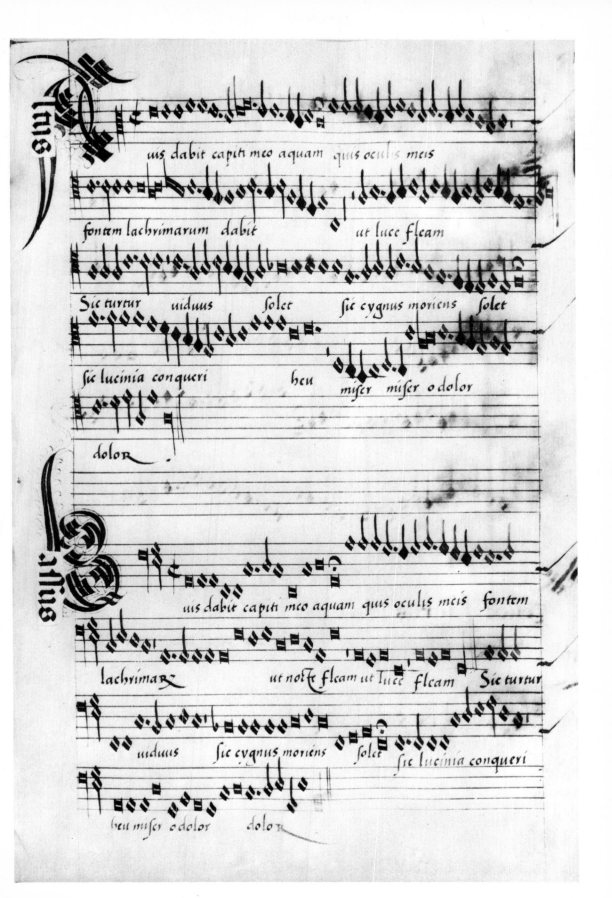

As the 'reft turtle mourns his mate,
As sings the swan his coming fate,
As the sad nightingale complains,
I pour my anguish and my strains.
Ah, wretched, wretched, past relief;
Oh, grief beyond all other grief!

The love-poetry of Lorenzo and Poliziano has been impressed even on those who are unaware of its existence by Botticelli, whose two greatest pictures, the *Primavera* and the *Birth of Venus*, were deliberately intended as illustrating it and whose portrayal of the beautiful girl whose death all Florence had mourned, as the holder of Venus's cloak, is a perpetual reminder of the beginning of Lorenzo the Magnificent's quest for love and poetry.

Illumination from a manuscript Codex Squarcialupi, *a book of Italian songs and music.*

Lorenzo Succeeds His Father

Almost before the wedding-festivities were over Lorenzo left Florence for Milan to deputise for his father at the christening of the infant son of Galeazzo Sforza and his wife, Bona of Savoy. Piero was particularly anxious to ensure that Milan remained faithful to the friendship which Cosmo de' Medici and Francesco Sforza had initiated and which they, as their fathers' sons, had continued. Lorenzo seemed the ideal person to send to Milan, were it not that Piero, dying, needed him more than ever by his side and, in the critical state of Italian politics, also wished to keep the personal and the diplomatic aspects of the mission safely segregated. As he saw it, it was important that Lorenzo was regarded as the representative of the family, not as an accredited envoy of Florence.

On the journey to Milan, however, Lorenzo found it impossible to avoid public occasions and to maintain the retirement and semi-privacy which Piero had enjoined.

At Lucca he was dragged from his modest lodgings outside the walls at 'The Crown' to attend a ceremonial High Mass, a public meeting and a banquet. At Pietra Santa, 'The Bell' where he was staying was similarly invaded by citizens who gave him a supper party in a green arbour overlookin the sea. He next visited Sarzana, which his father, two years earlier, had bought for Florence, in order to form his own opinion as to whether its position made it a good strategic bargain. It is possible that he may have openly expressed his opinions on it for, on receiving a report on the journey, Piero at Careggi wrote to Lucrezia, who was superintending affairs in Florence: 'You know how reluctantly I allowed Lorenzo to go; tell him that he is not an ambassador and is not to depart from his strict instructions and not to indulge in so many fictions. I am quite determined that the gosling shall not lead the gander to the water.'

Of the baptismal ceremony at Milan itself, Lorenzo has left one of his typically terse descriptions: 'I was much honoured, more indeed than any of the other sponsors, even though they were above me in dignity. I presented the Duchess with a gold chain and a large diamond which had cost about 3000 gold florins. The result was that the Duke asked me to stand sponsor for all his other children!'

Shortly after Lorenzo's return to Florence his father died. Of this event his 'notice' runs: 'Piero our father died on December 2 [3] 1469, at the age of fifty-three, after long and painful sufferings from gout. He did not wish to make a will, but after his death an inventory was made which showed an amount of 237,982 *scudi* as was proved by the memorandum made by my hand on page 32 of our large green parchment-book. He was buried in San Lorenzo where we are now erecting a tomb, as worthy as we can devise, for the reception of his mortal remains and those of his brother Giovanni. May God grant mercy to their souls! His loss was sincerely mourned by the whole town, for he was a just man and of great kindness of heart. The princes of Italy, especially the greater ones, consoled us by letters of condolence and embassies and offered their assistance for our protection.'

Piero's tomb, which was the work of Andrea Verrocchio, was not completed for three years and was thus described by Vasari: 'A sarcophagus of porphyry borne at the corners by bronze supports with beautifully turned leaves, and placed between the chapel of the Sacrament [dedicated to Ss. Cosmas and Damian] and the sacristy. There is no better work of bronze anywhere, especially as Verrochio had at the same time demonstrated his skill by arranging the tomb in the opening of a window, placed upon a pedestal and separating the chapel of the Sacrament from the Old Sacristy. To fill the gap between the sarcophagus and the vaulting he made a grille of bronze rope netting, diamond pattern, ornamented in places with festoons and other fancies, executed with great skill, judgment and invention. It would not be possible to discover a more perfectly executed work, whether cast or chiselled.'

It was, indeed, a triumph of simplicity and taste as worthy as was Botticelli's *Fortitude* to memorialise the simple, self-effacing invalid who held the interim between a great father and a greater son. It may be, as one of the historians of Florence expressed it, that 'if Piero il Gottoso had only been known as the father of Lorenzo de' Medici, it would have been a sufficient title to the gratitude of posterity.' But the truer verdict is that Lorenzo owed much, if not most, of his greatness to his father's quiet caretaking of his inheritance.

Lorenzo, at least, thought so. 'On the second day after my father's death',

Opposite: *The tomb of Piero de' Medici, Lorenzo's father, designed by Andrea Verrocchio, in the church of San Lorenzo.*

he recorded, 'the most distinguished men of the State and of the ruling party came to our house to request me to undertake the conduct of affairs in the city and government in the way that my father and grandfather had done. As such

Part of a fresco by Cigoli in the Palazzo Vecchio: left to right, *Michelangelo, Lorenzo the Magnificent, his brother Giuliano, and Leonardo da Vinci.*

a responsibility seemed too great for my inexperience (I was only twenty-one), and involved so much labour and so many dangers, I accepted it unwillingly and only for the sake of our friends and fortune, for those who are shut out of political influence have a bad position in Florence. Hitherto all has succeeded to the general honour and satisfaction, not in consequence of my wisdom, but by God's grace and by reason of the wise measures of my predecessors.'

The Florentine historian, Francesco Guicciardini, who was nine when Lorenzo died (his greater rival, Machiavelli, was twenty) gave this account of the nature of the Medici influence: 'It was a government usurped by the party, preserved by tyranny, neither violent nor cruel except in a few cases in which they were constrained by necessity, but founded upon the policy of favouring the lower classes, uniting the interests of the stronger with their own interests and suppressing all who seemed inclined to go their own way. As the power passed from father to son, the memory of ancient rivalry and enmity lived on. The Medici had always more their private advantage at heart than the general good, but as they had neither any position nor Signoria abroad, their interest was usually one with that of the Republic, whose glory and fame were likewise theirs. But even with so keen-sighted a man as Lorenzo, such a position might easily lead to errors, and he did in fact make mistakes in important cases to the disadvantage of the State, either by allowing himself to be carried away by passion or by regarding only his personal position and advantage, always under the pretext that his greatness and that of his family was necessary to the common good.'

Lorenzo's first care was to ratify and strengthen the Triple Alliance which, as he saw it, safeguarded Florence in relation to the rest of Italy – that between Florence, Milan and Naples. His own personal friendships with Sforza and Ferrante made this the easier and in the early spring of 1471 Sforza and Bona, his wife, visited Florence in state to discuss the political alignment. The occasion exceeded in splendour anything that had yet been seen in Italy. A hundred knights and five hundred foot soldiers formed the personal guard of the Duke and Duchess of Milan who themselves were lodged at Lorenzo's personal expense in the Medici palace, while their suite, in which even the kitchen-boys and grooms wore cloth of silver, velvet and silk, was entertained at the public cost by the *Signoria*.

The city was kept perpetually *en fête* with banquets, dances, horse-races in the streets and religious plays in three of the churches. In the most spectacular of these, *The Descent of the Holy Spirit* in the Church of Santo Spirito, the tongues of fire in some way got out of hand, the woodwork of the church was ignited and the whole building practically destroyed, including the rich thirteenth-, fourteenth- and early fifteenth-century decorations and Brunelleschi's masterpiece, the *Magdalen*. Though the Duke of Milan headed the subscription list for the restoration of the church with a gift of two thousand gold florins the gesture did nothing to endear him to the Florentines, who

Opposite: *Gerolamo da Vicenza's painting* The Death and Assumption of the Virgin, *based on a dramatisation within a church, of the type that led to the burning of Santo Spirito in Florence in 1471.*

regarded the fire as an evil omen and who, in any case, detested the Milanese visitors (who, as Machiavelli reported, though it was Lent, ate animal food daily 'without respect for God or His Church').

The Duke himself spent much time in his host's palace examining the treasures the Medici had collected there and he had at least the grace to concede, before he left, that however impressive his own splendours, they were outshone by Lorenzo's.

In the summer of that year 1471 Pope Paul II died and was succeeded on the Papal throne by the fifty-four-year-old Franciscan who, as a poor boy, had adopted the name of della Rovere and now, not without suspicion of simony, was able to change it for Sixtus IV. Of him it has been said that he was 'the first Pope who for the sake of founding a family sacrificed every interest of the Church and waded deep in crime and bloodshed for this purpose'. Although he was later to attempt to organise, in pursuance of his ends, the assassination of Lorenzo, there was nothing but cordiality on the occasion of their first meeting when Lorenzo was sent, as one of an embassy of six, by the *Signoria* of Florence, to congratulate him on his elevation to the Papacy.

Lorenzo's own account of the visit runs: 'In the month of September 1471 I was sent as ambassador to Rome on the occasion of the coronation of Pope Sixtus and was received very honourably. I brought from thence the two marble busts of Augustus and Agrippa which the Pope presented to me; and besides a chalcedony vase, and many cameos and other things purchased by myself.' Lorenzo was permitted to buy these cheaply, as they were part of the great collection which Sixtus IV's predecessor had amassed and in which Sixtus's only interest was to turn them into cash as quickly as possible.

The Pope also appointed the Medici bank in Rome as official treasurer to the Holy See and made new concessions in regard to the Medici share in the farming of the alum works at Tolfa. There was also the suggestion that Lorenzo's young brother, Giuliano, should be made a cardinal, but while this was treated seriously enough by Lorenzo, who would have welcomed a representative in the Sacred College in Rome, Sixtus had no intention of ever granting it. Cardinalates were for his own family.

William Roscoe, in his life of Lorenzo (published in 1796), has expressed the matter with an admirable succinctness which has eluded his biographical

Opposite: *Pope Sixtus IV 'who for the sake of founding a family sacrificed every interest of the Church'. In this fresco by Melozzo da Forli, he is shown giving audience, and two of his illegitimate Riario sons are chatting on the left.*

Overleaf: *A view of Rome in the fifteenth century: anonymous painting.*

DOMVM EXPOSITIS: VICOS FORA MOENIA PONTES:
NEAM TRIVII QVOD REPARARIS AQVAM.
LICET NAVTIS STATVAS DARE COMMODA PORTVS:
TICANVM CINGERE SIXTE IVGVM:
MEN VRBS DEBET: NAM QVAE SQVALORE LATEBAT:

successors: 'Sixtus IV at the time he ascended the pontifical chair had several sons, upon whom, in the character of "nephews" he afterwards bestowed the most important offices and the highest dignities of the Church. The indecency of Sixtus in thus lavishing upon his spurious offspring the riches of the Roman See, could only be equalled by their profuseness in dissipating them. Pietro, in whose person were united the dignities of the Cardinal of S. Sisto, Patriarch of Jerusalem and Archbishop of Florence, expended at a single entertainment given at Rome, 20,000 gold florins.'

That historic banquet was in honour of Ferrante's daughter given as part of Sixtus's policy of detaching Naples from the alliance with Florence. It did not take place for eighteen months or so after Lorenzo's return from Rome; but already the Pope's master-plan was decided on – to gain Naples's support, by making Ferrante King of Lombardy, to aid Pietro with men and money to make himself master of Rome and become Pope. Sixtus would willingly resign the Papacy to his passionately loved son, and thus make it hereditary. Whether or not such a scheme could ever have succeeded is questionable in the extreme – as one historian has expressed it, 'irresponsible power unhinged to some extent the faculties of Sixtus's mind and it is charitable to hope that he was not quite sane' – but that the Pope had in reality the intention of breaking the Triple Alliance, whereas Lorenzo was under the impression that he was a friend and ally, suggests that Lorenzo's lack of years was in fact a great drawback at this period.

And, as if to confirm such a judgment, he returned to Florence to confront another problem of which his handling was indubitably inept – the affair of Volterra.

Opposite: *The* Farnese *bowl, second-century Alexandrian art depicting the allegory of the Nile, was bought by Lorenzo the Magnificent in Rome in 1471.*

Volterra

Volterra, standing two thousand feet above sea-level, is about thirty miles south-west of Florence. In 1361, its citizens, tired of unceasing feuds among themselves, had voluntarily invited Florence to assume suzerainty, and the Republic now endeavoured to rule the unbiddable mountain people through a prefect, the resident *Capitano*, who was changed every six months, and by the exaction of an annual tribute. No sooner had the Volterrans agreed to this arrangement than they began to resent it and in less than a century they had made four rebellions against the régime they had imposed upon themselves.

A few miles to the south of Volterra is the hill of Castelnuova where deposits of alum had long been known to exist and had been spasmodically mined. In 1470 a citizen of Siena applied to the Volterran authorities for permission to float a company to mine systematically for alum, hoping to break the Papal-Medici monopoly at Tolfa. In return for the concession the company would pay an annual rental to the General Council of Volterra. Of the members of the company, three were Florentines, three Sienese and two, the wealthy oligarchs, Paolo Inghirami and Benedetto Riccobaldi, Volterrans. Immediately the contract was signed the citizens of Volterra, led by Francesco Caruggi, a champion of republican liberty and Inghirami's bitter enemy, protested against the alienation of public property from the municipality into private hands and, despite the company's offer of a higher rent, the alum mine was declared to be the property of the town and the contract adjudged not only a gross violation of the rights of the whole body but also illegal inasmuch as the vote had not been unanimous, as in the case of the sale or lease of common property it had to be.

The company's answer was to take possession of the mine by force.

A new commission of twelve citizens was then appointed by the Volterran

Opposite: *The countryside round Volterra.*

Signoria to probe the whole matter. In the meantime the mine was forcibly closed and all working suspended until Florence, in the person of Lorenzo, had given its verdict. To no one's surprise, Lorenzo found for the company.

The matter, in comparison with the great events of the time, may seem of small importance, but in its principles and its consequences, it is the crux of any estimate of Lorenzo's character. From that day to this it has excited passionate partisanship and the latest detailed examination of the episode is as recent as 1948. 'It has cast a slur on his name which cannot be obliterated', writes an historian as if to answer one of 1909 who mentions it only because 'Lorenzo's conduct has been so grossly distorted by his detractors that the episode has to receive notice'. Writers in the centuries between have tended to a naiveté of judgment in separating the political from the financial and exonerating Lorenzo on the grounds that he was not personally one of the three Florentine representatives of the company, whereas it is beyond doubt that it was in his business interest that the alum should be in the hands of his friends Inghirami and Riccobaldi. To say, as one biographer does, that 'it is extremely doubtful if he was connected with the alum company', because he was not one of the three, shows a strange misreading of the ways of fifteenth-century Florence or, indeed, the facts of political life in any age. On the other hand, one can partially excuse Lorenzo on the grounds of his youth – he was twenty-three – his inexperience and his delusions of grandeur arising from his imagined success with the Pope.

The return of Inghirami and Riccobaldi from Florence in triumph was the signal for the Volterran revolt. The two oligarchs were threatened with death and Inghirami took refuge in panic in the palace of the *Capitano*. The Volterran *Signoria* then summoned the *Capitano* to appear before them to discuss the situation and while he was so engaged the mob broke into his residence and, 'by an admixture of fire, smoke and sulphur', forced the fugitive from the room in which he was hiding, killed him and threw his dead body from an upstair window into the square below.

Thereupon the rights in the mines were officially transferred to the municipality, Lorenzo's verdict was set aside, a special Committee of Ten was formed with plenary power to secure the rights of the town from further infringement and a deputation sent to Florence to explain the terms on which Volterra would remain within the Republic. These terms included a pardon for the murders of Inghirami and his supporters, the return of Volterran hostages who had been sent to Florence by the *Capitano* and the recognition of the mines as the property of the Volterran municipality. Were these implemented, Volterra would resume her allegiance.

The debate on acceptance in the Florentine *Signoria* was long and bitter. Lorenzo's uncle-by-marriage, Tommaso Soderini (he had married Lucrezia

Tornabuoni's sister), to whom the dying Piero had commended the political education of Lorenzo and Giuliano and who had secured the recognition of Lorenzo rather than himself as the head of state, proposed that the Volterran terms should be agreed to. He pointed out that the real danger of the revolt lay not so much in Volterra itself as in the strain it might impose on the Triple Alliance. It was certain that the Volterrans would appeal for aid to Milan or to Naples or to the Pope, or possibly to all three, and in the changing political scene anything might happen. 'Better a lean peace than a fat victory', said Tommaso Soderini, to the approval of the majority of the *Signoria*. It was at this point that Lorenzo again intervened. His original wrong of assigning the mine to the company might have been righted but again personal considerations overcame those of statesmanship and justice. He was angry and he was afraid. His friends had been murdered, his judgment had been repudiated, the Florentine exiles had been invited to make common cause with the Volterrans to overthrow his house. Volterra, he ordered, must make unconditional surrender. If it did not he would reduce it, as a rebellious dependency, by force of arms. He engaged as his *condottiere* Federigo, Duke of Urbino, asking him to bring five thousand men to the attack and instructing him to finish the business as quickly as possible. He refused to listen to the pleas of the Bishop of Volterra urging that the well-disposed citizens of the town could easily restore order without recourse to arms. Lorenzo remained inflexible and Federigo, paid a hundred thousand golden florins from the Florentine state dowry fund, moved with great promptitude and captured a commanding position from which he could bombard the town. After twenty-five days the Volterrans realised that their position was hopeless and sent an embassy to treat with him.

While negotiations were still in progress a Volterran constable treacherously opened one of the gates to the besiegers and, on the night of June 17, 1472, the whole of Federigo's army of mercenaries made its way into the town, which was subjected to the most terrible sack which so far had ever been known in any war in Italy.

The sequel was what might have been expected. The Volterrans were deprived of all their rights, the mines were declared the property of Florence, a new fortress was built on the ruins of the church of S Pietro and the Bishop's palace so that no subsequent revolt should ever be possible, Federigo of Urbino was presented with a silver helmet and the citizenship of Florence and Lorenzo visited Volterra where he headed a subscription list for the restoration of the town with a carefully calculated but moderate donation.

As for the mines themselves, they fell into disuse on account of technical difficulties and, though Lorenzo made an effort to rework them when the

Pope revoked the agreement on the Tolfa alum, they were finally abandoned ten years after the sack of Volterra on the grounds that their produce did not justify the expense of working.

After the overthrow of the Volterrans, a new fort was built on the ruins of the church of San Pietro.

The Platonic Academy

In 1474, Lorenzo was visited by King Christian of Denmark, who has been uniformly described by writers on the Medici as an old man with a long white beard taking a pilgrimage to Rome in fulfilment of a vow. It may of course have been so, but as Christian at the time was thirty-eight and at the height of his powers as a soldier and diplomat who had united the crowns of Denmark, Norway and Sweden under his own rule, thanks to the influence of the Church and the financial backing of the Hanseatic League, it sounds improbable. Nor does the praise implied in the comment that 'his modest retinue contrasted with the Milanese and the wiser heads in Florence commented with approval of his dignity and simplicity' accurately suggest the truth that Christian, besides being deeply in debt to his backers, was an impoverished and extravagant man, chronically hard up and prepared to raise money by methods which were usually undignified and often unscrupulous.

In all probability Christian's visit to Lorenzo was connected with finance, as the power of the merchant-princes of the Hansa was just beginning to decline; and it was certainly to do with his plans for founding the University of Copenhagen, which he managed to accomplish before Lorenzo's death. The one episode for which the meeting of the two rulers was remembered does not unfairly epitomise it. Christian, having been received with great splendour, asked if he might be favoured with a sight of the celebrated copy of the Gospels in Greek which the Medici had obtained some years before from Constantinople and of the *Pandects* of Justinian. The Dane's welcome curiosity was gratified and, through his interpreter, he gave it as his opinion that such things constituted the real treasure of princes.

Not only would Lorenzo have agreed with him, but posterity has endorsed the judgment. Burckhardt, in his classic *The Civilization of the Renaissance in Italy* has expressed it memorably: 'If we seek to analyse the charm which the Medici, especially Cosmo the Elder and Lorenzo the Magnificent, exercised over Florence and over all their contemporaries we shall find that

131

it lay less in their political capacity than in their leadership in the culture of the age. To Cosmo belongs the special glory of recognising in the Platonic philosophy the fairest flower of the ancient world of thought.

'The famous band of scholars which surrounded Lorenzo was united together and distinguished from all other circles of the kind by this passion for a higher and idealistic philosophy. Lorenzo was not, indeed, a man of universal mind, but of all the great men who have striven to promote and favour spiritual interests few certainly have been so many-sided and in none probably was the inner need to do so equally deep.'

Lorenzo, indeed, was almost the perfect Platonist. Just as Plato's writings concern themselves with every aspect of life – politics, beauty, the laws of thought, education, love and friendship – yet never treat any specialised subject for its own sake, so Lorenzo related everything to the total personality and accepted Plato's criterion of Virtue as the overriding object of search. The intellectual approach to the knowledge of truth by the Socratic method of ironical questioning exactly suited his cast of mind, as, on another level, did his treatment of myths. Plato's definition of an Idea as a perfect and ideal pattern of which Reality is an imperfect copy appealed to Lorenzo the poet as surely as it appeals to all artists; and his formulation of a perfect state in the *Republic* enthralled Lorenzo the ruler. Above all was Plato's central paradox to challenge the liveliest of intellects – that philosophy itself was a mystical initiation which achieved for the chosen few by conscious enquiry what the Mysteries supplied to the vulgar by stirring up their emotions. The cleansing of the soul, the welcoming of Death, the ability to 'rage correctly' could be obtained by a training in dialectic, whose aim it was to purge the soul of error.

The Platonic Academy, which Cosmo, under the influence of Plethon, had founded at the beginning of the forties, was at its most influential with Lorenzo at the centre of it by the mid-seventies. The 'Father' of it was that Marsilio Ficino who had been originally appointed Lorenzo's tutor and given a secluded villa and farm at Montevecchio, near Careggi, which became the official headquarters of the Academy, where he worked on making an accurate translation of the entire works of Plato – a monumental project which he completed in 1491 at the age of fifty-eight.

In his later years he took Holy Orders and dedicated to Lorenzo a series of sermons on St Paul's Epistle to the Romans (into each of which he introduced references to Plato) to support his pupil-patron's quest for the key that should reconcile Platonism with Christianity. The essence of Ficino's Catholic

Opposite: *Part of Cosimo Rosselli's fresco, painted in 1486, which portrays:* left *Marsilio Ficino,* right *Pico della Mirandola.*

Cristoforo Landino, the Professor of Rhetoric in the Platonic Academy, from a fresco by Domenico Ghirlandaio.

belief was acceptance of the Incarnation. God became Man and the Incarnate Christ was God's masterpiece, His supreme work of art, presented as a model to be emulated. If this was a somewhat *simpliste* short-circuiting of careful theological safeguards, it had the merit – like Botticelli's use of the same model for Venus as for the Virgin Mary – of popularising the idea of comparative religion, from which all reconciliatory arguments must start.

After Ficino, the most useful member of the Academy was Lorenzo's other tutor, Cristoforo Landino, the Professor of Rhetoric, whose edition of Dante, published in 1481, illustrated another side of the Academy's work – the establishment of Dante, writing in the Tuscan tongue, as a classical poet worthy to take his place with Virgil and the Greeks in the European Pantheon. At the time of the visit of Christian of Denmark, Lorenzo was negotiating with Venice for the return of Dante's body to his native Florence and though he was unsuccessful he made the *amende* which was in his power of persuading the Florentine *Signoria* to annul the original decrees which had deprived Dante of his Florentine citizenship and solemnly to instal the poet's laurel-crowned statue in the Baptistery.

In addition to his fame as the editor of Dante, Cristoforo Landino was the recorder of some of the sessions of the Platonic Academy, and it is to him that posterity owes its knowledge of some of the Academy debates, including the occasion when nine members – including Lorenzo and his brother, Giuliano – accepted the hospitality of the Abbot of Camalduli, a few miles away. In Landino's *Disputationes Camaldulenses* is painted the retreat on the wooded heights of Casentino where the philosophers spent much of their time lying under the shadow of the great trees, with a spring babbling hard by in such surroundings as Virgil loved and discussing the Latin poet, the bridge between the Greeks and Dante. Was Virgil primarily a philosopher and only secondarily a poet? Was there, allegorically, a harmony between the teaching of Plato and Virgil? In what ways was the philosophical meaning beneath the surface of the text obvious to the ordinary reader?

Marsilio Ficino, who was now regarded as the high-priest of Platonism, had begun life as an Epicurean – a circumstance of which Poliziano kept teasingly reminding him and to which he himself paid equable tribute by insisting on keeping in his study a picture of the 'Laughing Philosopher', Democritus, defying the tears of the 'Dark Philosopher', Heraclitus. It reminded him and his visitors, so he said, that cheerfulness was a quality becoming to a philosopher. And he himself attempted to reconcile the Epicurean precepts that Pleasure (*Voluptas*) is the highest good by so redefining Pleasure in terms which could be accepted by the sternest Platonist. The fruition of knowledge is in pleasure, he wrote in his little treatise *Epistola de felicitate* addressed to Lorenzo, and therefore Pleasure and Joy, in a Platonic lover, are superior to enquiry and vision.

The painter of Ficino's picture was another member of the Platonic Academy, Leone Battista Alberti, who died in his late sixties in 1472, the

Overleaf: *Frontispiece of Cristoforo Landino's 1481 edition of Dante's work which established Dante as a classical poet on a par with Virgil and the Greeks.*

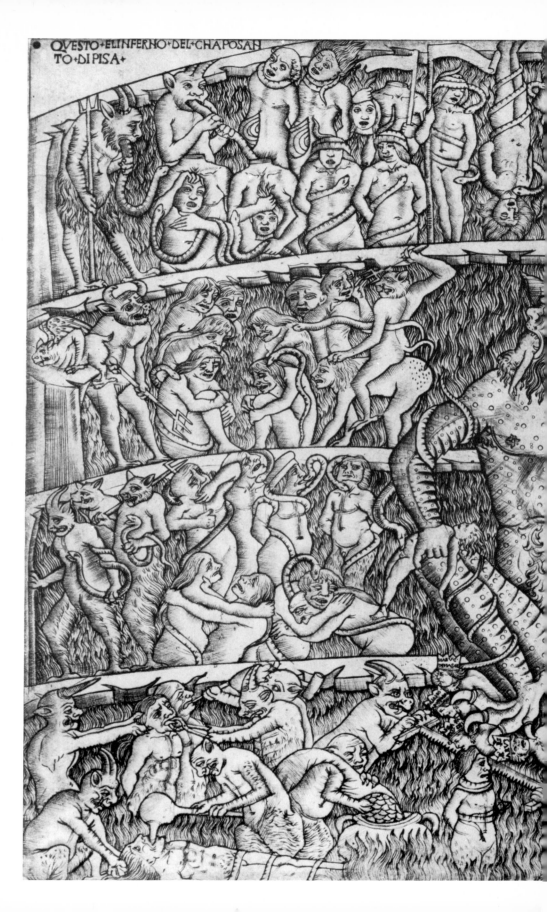

QVESTO+ELINFERNO+DEL+CHAPOSAN
TO+DI PISA+

year of the sack of Volterra. In one sense, Alberti might almost be considered the representative man of the Florentine Renaissance, in his all-embracing curiosity and aptitude for knowledge, his sensitivity to every charm, the realism of his pictures, the objectivity of his style and the urbanity of his Epicurean-Platonic spirit. On those who knew him, he produced the effect epitomised by Poliziano in his preface to Alberti's work on architecture, published after his death: 'Nothing, however abstruse in learning, however remote from the ordinary range of scholarship was hidden from his genius. One might question whether he was better fitted for oratory or for poetry, whether his speech was the more weighty or the more polished. Rightly to praise him is beyond my poor powers of eloquence.'

In another of his *Disputationes*, Cristoforo Landino records an argument between Alberti and Lorenzo. Alberti contended that the contemplative life, spent in the search for truth was the only goal worth striving for and that Lorenzo, called to the cares and responsibilities of active government must seize every opportunity to withdraw from participation in affairs to refresh his soul and regain his perspective in contemplation. Alberti then proceeded to the full extent of the Platonic doctrine and insisted that no one could hope to reach perfection as long as he permitted the cares of this world to divert him from the development of his own spiritual and intellectual qualities.

At that point Lorenzo interrupted with a question. What would happen to all communities if all the best men withdrew themselves on principle from the duties of government? Would it not follow that the State would have to be ruled by the worst men in it? Alberti replied that the best men could always assist the Government by their advice and so, by their counsel if not by their actions, could help the State. But the question whether the worst men, who had the responsibility of ruling, were likely to pay any attention to the best men who had refused that responsibility was ignored by Alberti.

Alberti, by reason of his age – he was born in 1405 – his many-sided genius, his energy and his great reputation was, in his day, the acknowledged oracle of culture and scholarship in Florence, and, particularly in his championship of the Tuscan vernacular, had as great an influence on Lorenzo as his two formal tutors, Ficino and Landino. Fifteen years before Lorenzo's birth, Alberti had, in one of his treatises, urged that 'even if men of learning boast of the authority possessed by the Latin language on the grounds that so many learned men have used it, the like honour will certainly be paid to

Opposite: *Self-portrait of the artist Leone Battista Alberti, who maintained that worldly cares must not divert the Platonist from the development of his own spiritual qualities.*

our language of today, if men of culture take pains to purify and polish it.'
Lorenzo and Poliziano became its leading practitioners and it would not be
unfair to see Alberti as in fact the moulder of the Platonic Academy who
saved it from mere scholarly pedantry. Meetings on Plato's supposed birthday
and the lamp kept always burning before his bust, and re-enactments of the
Symposium and arguments about the niceties of the philosopher's meaning
in disputed passages were stimulating enough to the scholarship of the élite,
and a sufficient tribute to Marsilio Ficino, its president; Cristoforo Landino's
work on Dante linked the far with the immediate past; Alberti's enthusiasm
and temperamental affinity with Virgil emphasised the continuity of Greece,

*Lorenzo the Magnificent with Mirandola, Poliziano, Pulci, Ficino, Landino,
Alberti and others : fresco by Vasari.*

Imperial Rome and mediaeval Florence, while it was left for Lorenzo and Poliziano to dominate the present and adumbrate the future in poems in the *Lingua Toscana.*

There was also, in the later years of the Academy, the young Pico, Count of Mirandola, who was fourteen years younger than Lorenzo and whose precocity was considered one of the marvels of the age. In the range of his speculation Pico della Mirandola surpassed his companions. He shared their passion to reconcile Platonism with Christianity, but he enlarged the boundaries of the search for a synthesis by introducing Hebrew and the mysteries of the Cabala. He learnt Hebrew, surrounded himself with Jewish teachers, such as the famous Eliah del Medigo and in his writings including

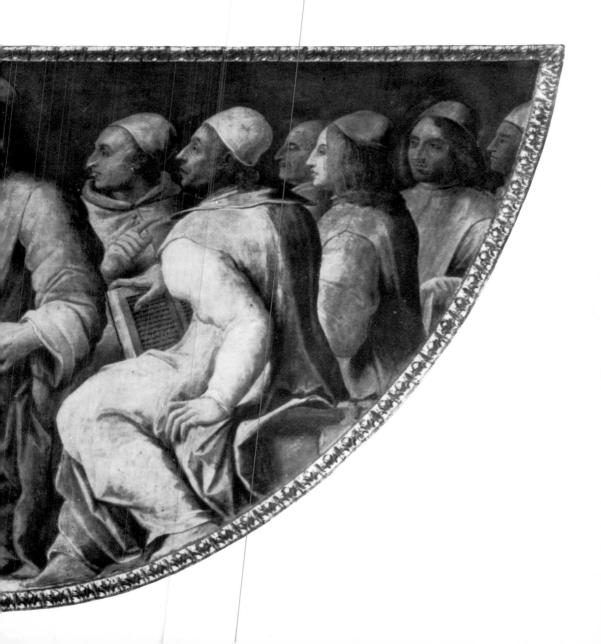

the famous *Conclusiones* (many of which were condemned by the Church)
incorporated much Cabalistic lore.

At the basis of the quest for ultimate unity, a system of fusing the doctrines
of Christianity, the teaching of the Greeks, the lore of the Hebrews and the
hidden speculations veiled in Orphism on the one hand and the Cabala on
the other, lay the theory of 'vestiges of the Trinity'. 'He that understands
clearly', wrote Pico in one of his *Conclusiones*, 'how the unity of Venus is
unfolded in the trinity of the Graces, and the unity of Necessity in the trinity
of the Fates and the unity of Saturn in the trinity of Jupiter, Neptune and
Pluto, knows the proper way of proceeding.' The central Christian doctrine,
that of the Holy Trinity, was, by many vestiges, to be discerned in the Greek
myths, philosophically interpreted. The discovery of 'triads' became something very like a mania. Not only in those which Pico della Mirandola had
mentioned – the three Graces, Chastity, Desire and Beauty (to translate the
untranslatable *Castitas, Voluptas, Pulchritudo*) as the attributes of the one
Venus, Goddess of Love and three Fates (who are not unrelated to the Graces)
as the attributes of Necessity – but even in details of the theology of the
Graces, the triad is to be discerned. 'The Trinity has left its mark on every
part of Divine Creation', as Marsilio Ficino wrote; and the bounty conferred
by the gods on lower beings was conceived as a king of overflowing (*emanatio*)
which produced a vivifying rapture or conversion (*vivificatio, raptio* or
conversio) whereby the lower beings were drawn back to Heaven to rejoin the
gods (*remeatio*). Thus, in the circle of grace, the triplicity of giving, accepting
and returning was perceptible; and the Graces themselves were so represented as to reveal to the initiated the Neoplatonic triad of procession, conversion and return.

Perhaps the most famous exposition of this doctrine was Botticelli's picture
painted for Lorenzo which is known as the *Primavera* and which is un-
intelligible without a knowledge of the doctrine. In the centre is Venus, the
One, contemplating her trinity of Graces, *Pulchritudo, Castitas* and *Voluptas*.
Above Venus is the blind Cupid aiming his arrow at *Castitas*. The Graces
are engaged in a dance and, as Professor Wind puts it, 'in so far as dialectic
can be danced, it has been accomplished in this group. "Opposition",
"Concord" and "Concord in Opposition", all three are expressed in the
postures and steps and in the articulate style of joining the hands. Placed
palm against palm to suggest an encounter but quietly interlocked in the
absence of conflict, they rise up high to form a significant knot when they
illustrate the Beauty of Passion.'

Another famous portrayal of the Graces made at this time was Pico della

Opposite: *The Three Graces: detail from Botticelli's* Primavera.

Mirandola's medal. Here the allegory is expressed in simpler terms than in Botticelli's detailed telling. The *Primavera* shows the middle Grace as *Castitas* on the point of being initiated by her sisters, *Voluptas* and *Pulchritudo*, into the fullness of Love. Chastity cannot escape Cupid's arrow, but the presiding presence of Venus, clothed, ensures that it is right that it should be so and the transformation is betokened by the fall of her garment from her left shoulder where *Voluptas* stands and, in deference to *Pulchritudo* on her right, a rich flowing tress escapes from the knot of her hair.

The Graces on Pico's medal take up the story at the point where the initiation of the *Primavera* has been accomplished and experience has changed *Castitas* into *Amor*. Round the edge of the medal is inscribed, so that there might be no mistaking, *Pulchritudo, Amor, Voluptas*, with *Amor* retaining the characteristic of *Castitas* of showing only her back to the beholder. The medal illustrates exactly the definition from Marsilio Ficino's treatise on Platonic love: 'Amor starts from Pulchritudo and ends in Voluptas', and the poses of the Graces illustrate the idea of *emanatio, raptio* and *remeatio*, with its reminder – to quote again from Marsilio's commentary on Plato's *Symposium* – that 'the Trinity was regarded by the Pythagorean philosophers as the measure of all things, the reason being, I surmise, that God governs things by threes and that the things themselves also are determined by threes.'

An extreme case of the triad finding mania was the so-called Three Marriages of St Anne (*Trinubium Annae*) which attempted to entangle St Anne, the Patroness of Florence, in the prevailing pattern. It was suggested that the three Marys of the Gospel story were all daughters of St Anne by three different husbands – the Virgin Mary by Joachim; Mary, the wife of Zebedee and the mother of James and John, by Salomas; and Mary, the wife of Alpheus and mother of Thaddeus, James the Less and Joseph Justus, by Cleophas. In the controversy which these speculations inspired among theologians, it was soon pointed out that it was as improper as it was unlikely to suppose that St Anne, having immaculately conceived the Virgin Mary, would subsequently have two other children by two other husbands, and Joachim was therefore designated her third and last instead of her first spouse.

This idea that St Anne (whose name in Hebrew means 'Grace') was successively the wife of three husbands and the mother of three daughters all named Mary was adopted by the artists even when it had been rejected by

Opposite: *The eleventh-century church of the Hermitage of Camalduli, the scene of some meetings of the Platonic Academy.*

the theologians and abandoned by the philosophers. Thus an incidental outcome of the Academy might be said to be the fashion for such paintings as Lorenzo di Pavia's *Holy Family* where in addition to the Virgin Mary, Joseph, Jesus and John the Baptist, are St Anne with three men, with their names inscribed as Joachim, Cleophas and Salomé, as well as their children and grandchildren, bringing the number of characters up to the satisfactory eighteen.

The influence of the Academy on European thought was so great – in one sense, the Academy *was* the Renaissance – that it tends to obscure the necessity of it to Lorenzo himself as a school of government in which he could study the history and principles of the classic past to aid him in the uncharted present. His situation as a ruler was unique. At the age of twenty he had been called on by a meeting of over six hundred of the most influential men of the Republic of Florence to continue the work which, for the last thirty-five years, his father and grandfather, as heads of the Medici had done for the city-state. This was to rule without the appearance of ruling. To appear as anything but a private citizen was, as his grandfather Cosmo had found, to invite exile under a constitution strictly and specifically framed to prevent any citizen gaining personal power. The mere unworkability of the constitution had indeed over the years allowed in practice an intelligent laxity which was not recognised in theory; but it remained true that, in the last analysis, the Medici, whatever their wealth, influence and reputation, could rely on nothing but good-will.

Lorenzo's authority was not hereditary nor could it be transmitted by descent. No civil list was voted for its upkeep. It had no armed force at its disposal to enforce policy. Lorenzo not only could not initiate any legislation but he could not even veto measures of which he disapproved. And because of the necessary emphasis on his private citizenship, there was no elaborate etiquette which might have gone some way to providing an atmosphere of 'the divinity which doth hedge a king'.

Lorenzo had thus to devise his own pattern of sovereignty and provide his own methods of exercising and maintaining it. The manipulation of ballot-boxes, of councils and of committees, the pulling of political wires and expertise in bribery, the provision of bread and circuses – all the appurtenances of democracy, in fact, Lorenzo studied in the democracy of Athens and the republicanism of Rome. And there, too, he could learn to beware of the calumny which could represent all attempts at imposing order as 'tyranny' and an attack on 'liberty'.

Towards the end of his life, Lorenzo wrote for the edification and instruction of his children, a morality play, *La Rappresentazione di S. Giovanni e S Paolo*. In it he asks what a prince is worth who is not obeyed by his own subjects, especially at the beginning for the head of a government must make his position secure within the first four days.

> *Che val signor che obedito non sia*
> *Da suoi soggetti, e massimo allo inizio?*
> *Perchè un rettor d'una podesteria*
> *Ne' primi quattro di fa il suo ofizio.*

And that he himself, in a situation not of his choosing but from which, in the circumstances, there was no escape, was able so to act was due to his training from his earliest years in the history and philosophy of the classic governments as seen and expounded and debated by the members of the Platonic Academy.

Pico della Mirandola's medal, on the verso of which are depicted the Three Graces.

Lorenzo's Brother

When Lorenzo assumed the burden of governing Florence, his brother, Giuliano, was sixteen. On their father's death, there had been some talk of the brothers sharing power, but this idea was soon abandoned partly because of the political dangers inseparable from dual control, partly because of Giuliano's youth, partly because there was no doubt in anyone's mind that, whatever the theory, Lorenzo and Giuliano would in fact work as one. What might be called the 'two-brother tradition' of the Medici, sanctified by Cosmas and Damian, manifested in the partnership of Cosmo and his brother Lorenzo, and spectacularly continued in Piero and his brother Giovanni, reached a climax of identity in Lorenzo and Giuliano. Brought up in the Medici palace, the boys almost repeated the pattern of the sickly elder and the competent and compelling younger, except that Lorenzo had not Piero's physical weakness nor Giuliano Giovanni's organisational ability. But Lorenzo was one to whom, as one observer put it, 'in exterior bodily gifts, Nature had proved a stepmother', with his large but ill-proportioned body, his sallow complexion and his ugly features, the curiously shaped nose which had no sense of smell, the near-sighted, peering eyes and the harsh repellent voice, 'That he was ugly in a marked degree cannot be questioned' runs one estimate; 'all the masculine beauty of the family was usurped by Giuliano.'

And Giuliano, tall and admirably proportioned, with his sparkling eyes, his olive skin, his profusion of black curls, his easy athleticism, was not only the darling of Florence but, thanks to Botticelli's use of him as his model for Mercury in the *Primavera* and for Mars in his *Mars and Venus*, a European ideal of male beauty. He was, as her youngest child, his mother's favourite and from his earliest years had been accustomed to having his portrait painted at her request in various religious pictures so that his beauty was emphasised by Lorenzo's plainness, as in the early representation of the brothers, as Cosmas and Damian, worshipping the Christ-Child.

Yet Lorenzo had no jealousy of him, as Giuliano had nothing but extrava-

An illustration entitled La Giostra di Giuliano de Medici *from a late fifteenth-century edition of Poliziano's* Stanze.

gant loyalty to Lorenzo. Poliziano was never tired of insisting on the ideal relationship that existed between the brothers. They were as one, each, as in previous generations of Medici brothers devoting himself to becoming the complement of the other. And in the 'bread and circuses' aspect of the government, it was Giuliano who undertook the provision and organisation of the splendid spectacles and opulent occasions which were a required and expected part of Lorenzo's rule.

The most magnificent of the spectacles was the tournament held in Giuliano's honour in the Piazza di Santa Croce some time in 1475. (The usual date given is January 28 but, as this is the depth of winter, it is probably a mistake for June 28 which fell within the octave of the feast of St John the Baptist, the week in which Florence was always *en fête* for its patron saint. The Florentine year, indeed, pivoted on this week. On one occasion Lucrezia Tornabuoni, who was taking the baths at Morbo, wrote to Lorenzo: 'I am making a short stay without ceremonies, in order to be in Florence by Monday, St John's Eve. Send me the horses when you like so long as they are here by June 19.')

But whether 'Giuliano's Tournament' occurred in winter or summer, it seems to have eclipsed in splendour even 'Lorenzo's Tournament' of seven years earlier. Lorenzo's motto was still *Le Temps Revient*, while Giuliano's standard announced, as it were, the 'book' of the tournament. On the standard was a figure of Pallas, in a golden tunic and bearing lance and shield, while Cupid was shown bound to the stump of an olive tree on a flowery meadow, with bow and broken arrows at his feet.

The poem on this tournament did not, as we have seen, attempt to give, as Pulci's poem on 'Lorenzo's Tournament' had given, a blow-by-blow description of the event. Indeed Poliziano is hardly concerned with actuality in his fourteen-hundred line *Stanze della Giostra di Giuliano de' Medici* whose theme is Giuliano's resistance to the assaults of Love and Love's final victory. The *Stanze* have been well described as 'this lovely idyll of Renaissance Florence and a tribute to Lorenzo's achievements as its leader', dedicated to 'Laurel of happy birth beneath whose shade Florence rests joyful and at peace'.

After a tribute to Lorenzo, Angelo Poliziano proceeds to a description of Giuliano and a lament that he refuses to surrender his heart to a woman.

Giuliano de' Medici was the model for Mars in Botticelli's painting Mars and Venus.

As Roscoe translates it,

> For Julian many a maiden heaved the sigh
>   And many a glance the tender flame confess'd;
> But not the radiance of the brightest eye
>   Could melt the icy rigour of his breast.
> Wild through the trackless woods the youth would hie,
>   Severe of aspect and disdaining rest;
>   While the dark pine or spreading beech supplied
>   A wreath, from summer suns his head to hide.
>
> When evening star its milder lustre lends
>   The wanderer to his cheerful home retires,
> There every muse his loved return attends,
>   And generous aims and heavenly verse inspires;
> Deep through his frame the sacred song descends,
>   With thirst of ancient praise his soul that fires;
>   And Love, fond trifler, mourns his blunted dart
>   That harmless flies where Dian shields the heart.

Giuliano then reproaches the weakness of those who are in thrall to love –
rather in the manner in which, in later classical poems, Adonis lectures
Venus – and goes off to the chase, which gives Poliziano an opportunity to
demonstrate his descriptive talents.

Love, who feels his divinity insulted by Giuliano's attitude, has recourse
to a stratagem. A beautiful white hind suddenly appears and crosses the
hunter's path. He pursues it but it eludes all his endeavours to wound it and
his efforts lead him far from his companions. When his horse is almost
exhausted, a nymph makes her appearance and Giuliano, overcome by her
beauty, forgets the chase and accosts her with trepidation and amazement.
Her reply completes her triumph. Evening falls and Giuliano returns home,
pensive and alone.

There follows a lengthy description of the court of Venus in the island of
Cyprus. Cupid returns thither to recount his success to Venus, his mother,
and she, to enhance the value of the conquest, desires Giuliano to proclaim
his surrender to love by holding a tournament. The whole band of loves
consequently repairs to Florence and Giuliano prepares for the combat. In a
dream sent by Venus, he seems to be victor in the joust and on his return,
crowned with laurel and olive, his beloved appears to him, but is soon
enveloped in a thick cloud and disappears from his sight. This incident is
interpreted by Poliziano as meaning the death of the beautiful Simonetta, the
wife of Marco Vespucci, who was reputed to be Giuliano's mistress and
who died suddenly the following year to the grief of all Florence. Some
consolatory verses are then addressed to the bereaved lover who, awaking
from his dream, invokes Minerva to crown his life with glory. Here, abruptly,
the poem ends.

It will be seen at once that Botticelli's three masterpieces – *the Birth of
Venus*, the *Primavera* and *Mars and Venus* can be regarded as illustrations
to the poem. (For the sake of any reader interested in the minutiae of the
matter they are stanzas 100 and 101 for the *Birth of Venus*; stanzas 122 and
123 for *Mars and Venus*; and scattered passages throughout the whole
poem for the *Primavera* which shows the return of Venus and her court to
the City of Flowers.)

Apart from attempts at the identification of the various persons in the art
of the time (and the perpetual disagreement among various 'experts') there
is a wide range of speculation. Simonetta certainly did exist and as she was
known as *La Bella* and was the toast of Florence it is possible that she was
Giuliano's mistress. But as Giuliano was intended for the Cardinalate and so,

Opposite: *Piero di Cosimo's portrait of Simonetta Vespucci, who was thought
to have been Giuliano de' Medici's mistress.*

officially at least, dedicated to celibacy and as he, no less than his brother, was imbued with the ideals of Platonic love – one is tempted to assign to him the rôle of Alcibiades in the Academy's readings of Plato's *Symposium* – it seems reasonable to accept the thesis of Poliziano in his poem that he was notably indifferent to women.

After his death, he was, indeed, credited with a bastard son, but contemporary accounts of the child differ. Many asserted that the boy was born posthumously. According to others, an intimate friend about a year after his death informed Lorenzo of the child's existence and induced him to visit the mother, the daughter of a burgher, who persuaded Lorenzo to take the child and bring him up in the Palazzo Medici with his own children. Others, again, say that Lorenzo's action in doing this and naming the boy Giulio, was immediate and of his own volition. There is, in fact, no certainty, though there can be little doubt that Giulio (who became Pope Clement VII) showed no signs of inheriting Giuliano's charm, courage, magnanimity or looks.

A month or two after 'Giuliano's Tournament', the two brothers went to Pisa for a long visit connected with Lorenzo's restoration of the university there. The Medici owned a large house with a garden running down to the river, where Lorenzo often spent periods of retirement for months at a time. Pisa, the key to the Arno, had been acquired by Florence some years before Lorenzo's birth, but on the Pisan side there remained such resentment and bitterness at their loss of liberty that any true co-operation seemed impossible. Lorenzo, realising Florence's economic need of Pisa, had determined as soon as he came to power by friendship and conciliation to win Pisa to a willing allegiance. In pursuance of this policy, he not only made strenuous efforts to develop Pisa as a port, himself taking financial shares in the project, but he restored the University of Pisa by incorporating it with the University of Florence. The same statutes were to apply to both, but whereas Florence concentrated on the Humanities and Philosophy, Pisa was to specialise in Law.

During the April of 1476, the brothers were at Pisa when news arrived of Simonetta's illness. They sent the Medici physicians to offer their services, but, in the night between April 26 and April 27 *La Bella* died. Stories and legends accumulated round the circumstances. It is possible that Lorenzo and Giuliano were walking in their garden at Pisa when they suddenly noticed a

Opposite top: *Lorenzo and his brother Giuliano represented by Botticelli as the saints Cosmas and Damian worshipping the Christ-Child.*

Opposite bottom: *A detail from Fra Angelico's* Pala di San Marco *showing the burial of the saints Cosmas and Damian beside the convent and church of San Marco.*

new star, brighter than the rest, and knew that Simonetta was with the gods, and that her eyes were the source of the increased light. This was the conceit of Lorenzo's sonnet, *O chiara stella,* which Symonds has translated:

O lucid star that with transcendent light
    Quenchest of all those neighbouring stars the gleam,
    Why thus beyond thy usage doest thou stream,
Why art thou fain with Phoebus still to fight?

Haply those beauteous eyes, which from our sight
    Death stole, who now doth vaunt himself supreme,
    Thou hast assumed: clad with their glorious beam
Well may'st thou claim the sun-god's chariot bright.

Listen, new star, new regent of the day,
    Who with unwonted radiance fills our heaven,
O listen, goddess, to the prayers we pray!
    Let so much splendour from thy sphere be riven
That to these eyes which fain would weep alway,
    Unblinded, thy glad sight may yet be given.

It is possible, also, that a great mist arose and dimmed the stars and that there was a presage of menace in the air and an unaccountable unquiet in men's minds. But it is a fact of history that, exactly two years later, on April 26, 1478, Giuliano was assassinated.

In the early days of April 1476, however, the sky was clear enough and Poliziano, in one of his letters has left a description of the setting-out of the brothers and their companions on their thirty-five mile journey to Pisa: 'Yesterday (April 7), after leaving Florence we came as far as San Miniato, singing all the way, and occasionally talking of holy things so as not to forget Lent. At Lastra we drank *zappolino*, which tasted much better than I had been told. Lorenzo is brilliant and makes the whole company gay. Yesterday I counted twenty-six horses that are with him. When we reached San Miniato we began to read a little of St Augustine, but the reading resolved itself into music and looking at and instructing a certain well-known dancer who is here.'

The Pazzi Conspiracy

Eight months after Simonetta's death, there occurred in Milan another death which affected Lorenzo politically. On the feast of St Stephen, December 26, 1476, his friend and ally, Galeazzo Maria Sforza, Duke of Milan, was murdered, at the age of thirty-two, as he was entering the Church of St Stephen to attend the great annual High Mass commemorating the saint. The time and place had been carefully chosen by the assassins. As it was an ecclesiastical occasion, the Duke might be relatively unarmed. As it was a popular holiday, a considerable crowd of citizens might be expected to be there to witness a deed which the perpetrators believed would be regarded as an act of tyrannicide in the great classic tradition.

The three young murderers were all pupils of Cola Montano, a fashionable Humanist who has been well described as 'one of the cowardly literary agitators who never dare face the deeds to which they drive their scholars'. Of him, Machiavelli wrote: 'He discussed with them the faults of their Prince and the wretched state of his subjects and so worked upon their minds as to induce them to bind themselves by oath to destroy the Duke as soon as they were old enough to make the attempt.' Having decided to do the deed, the three, Visconti, Lampugnani and Olgiati, determined that it should be accomplished successfully and they met frequently for rehearsals. They took in turn different positions and struck each other with sheathed daggers, their blows being regulated by the position of the one who was acting as victim.

On the appointed day, as the Duke approached the door of the church, Lampugnani and Olgiati advanced towards him as if to clear the way for him. Then the former fell on one knee under pretence of presenting a petition to the Duke and struck him two blows in front quickly followed by two more

157

from the standing Olgiati. The Duke staggered forward, which gave the opportunity to Visconti to stab him behind in the shoulder and the spine. The Duke fell dead, calling on the name of Our Lady.

Of all men Galeazzo Maria Sforza, by his insatiable debauchery, his sadistic blood-lust, his treachery to his friends and by a general reputation which included the belief that he had, like his prototype Nero, murdered his own mother, might have seemed to deserve removal and to justify tyrannicide. The three soi-disant patriots waited for approving cries of 'Liberty!' 'The Republic!'; but all that happened was the immediate death of two of them at the hands of the infuriated populace and the capture and death of the third after his father had refused to hide him. No commotion whatever took place in the city and Galeazzo's seven-year-old son succeeded to the dukedom.

Whatever the appearance of temporary stability gained by the widowed Duchess Bona's acting as Regent for her son, Gian (he whose baptism Lorenzo had attended), all Italy knew that it could not last. The murdered Duke had five brothers of whom the most ruthless and energetic was Ludovico, known, because of his swarthy appearance as Il Moro, the Moor. They had no intention of allowing their sister-in-law to continue in the Regency and it was obvious that for years Milan, hitherto so strong and stable, would be unpredictable and weak. No one was more affected than Lorenzo, because the Milanese alliance was the keystone of Medici policy and, whichever faction prevailed there, must remain so. But henceforth Milan would probably have to rely on Florentine strength rather than the reverse, in addition to Florence, for some time at least, having to back both candidates.

Lorenzo immediately instructed Tommaso Soderini, who was his ambassador in Milan, to assure the Duchess Bona of his continued support, and at the same time he showed Ludovico, whom Bona had banished to Pisa, the utmost consideration and kindness which stood him in good stead when Ludovico eventually took control of Milan in the autumn of 1479 and became, for all practical purposes the reigning Duke.

Some of Lorenzo's contemporaries blamed him 'for neither desiring nor seeking the peace and safety of Milan' and later liberal writers, imagining apparently that the code of a pious Sunday-school superintendent should have been adopted to rule quattrocento Florence, accuse him not only of self-interest but of 'double dealing'.

The turn of events at Milan inevitably affected the Pope's plans for the breaking of the Florence-Naples-Milan alliance and the overthrow of Lorenzo so that he and his Riario 'nephews' might gain control of all Italy. Lorenzo's

Opposite: *Portrait by Piero del Pollaiolo of the sadistic and treacherous Galeazzo Maria Sforza, Duke of Milan.*

present weakness suggested that this was the moment for throwing off the mask of friendship and making an open attack. Consequently Sixtus transferred the lucrative Papal account from the Medici bank to that of their financial rivals, the Pazzi.

The Pazzi were one of the oldest and most powerful families of Florence. Pazzo de Pazzi was a companion of Godfrey de Bouilon when, on the crusade of 1099, Jerusalem was captured. Pazzo brought back to Florence a fragment of Christ's tomb. From this sacred stone was struck, every Easter Eve, the new fire on the High Altar of the cathedral. From the sparks was ignited a firework in the form of a dove known as the Colombina. This was carried to the Pazzi car which, packed with fireworks, had been placed on the piazza between the Baptistery and the Duomo. At a touch Florence was bathed in light to signify and to welcome the Resurrection. The *Carro de' Pazzi* had by Lorenzo's day become one of the great solemnities of Florence and alone was enough to make a household word of the family which had been famous before the Medici were ever heard of.

Andrea de' Pazzi, the head of the house in the days of Cosmo de' Medici, further ennobled it by receiving a knighthood from King René of Provence, whose agent he was, but he subsequently repudiated it and became enrolled as a burgher to enable himself to hold political and public office. The head of the Pazzi in Lorenzo's day was Jacopo who, according to Poliziano, sweated his work people and frequently withheld their wages with the result that he was generally disliked. Poliziano, indeed, asserted that neither he nor his ancestors had at any time been genuinely popular in Florence, but this can hardly have been true and probably reflects Poliziano's personal prejudices. And, as one of the Pazzi family had married Lorenzo's sister, Bianca, the two houses, despite financial rivalry, were personally on friendly enough terms for the Pazzi to be regarded as devoted to the interests of the Medici ascendancy.

Jacopo's nephew, Francesco, 'a man of great arrogance and pretensions' could never understand why the Medici were preferred by the citizens of Florence to his own family. He lost no opportunity of traducing them and lived chiefly in Rome because he said there was no room for him in Florence as long as the Medici were there. His jealous hatred was increased by Lorenzo's interference in the matter of his brother, Giovanni's, estate. Giovanni de' Pazzi had married Beatrice Borromeo and when her father died, leaving no will, his estate under the existing law should have passed to her. Her Borromei cousins, however, laid claim to it and by the action of Lorenzo, so it was said (the evidence is not altogether clear), a retrospective law of

Opposite: *The Pazzi palace in Florence.*

intestacy was passed in 1476, under which the claims of females to the property of a father who had died intestate were set aside, the estate passing to male collaterals.

Such an action may not have been due to Lorenzo's interference, but there is no doubt that the Pazzi believed it was and Machiavelli in his history of the times is precise in stating that this act of injustice – for it was 'a law made for the occasion, contrary to custom and the just tenor of laws, which should apply to the future' – was the cause of the Pazzi's hatred of the Medici. Even Giuliano de' Medici thought that his brother was going too far and feared that by grasping at too much he might lose everything.

The Pazzi plot to overthrow Lorenzo and displace the Medici in Florence was hatched in Rome by Francesco, who was now in close touch with the Pope. Jacopo, in Florence, at first was 'colder than ice' toward the project. Another member of the family pointed out that it would be much safer to ruin Lorenzo, who momentarily was hard-pressed for money, by making him a loan at an impossibly high rate of interest. And the Pazzi who was Lorenzo's brother-in-law was kept in complete ignorance of the plan.

The chief movers in the project outside the family were the Pope and his favourite son, Girolamo Riario. Those historians who refer to it as the Papal-Pazzi plot are indeed correct in their emphasis. Francesco would certainly not have proceeded alone with it, as long as the head of his family, Jacopo, disapproved. Only when Girolamo Riario, with the Pope's consent, approached Francesco with the suggestion of murdering both the Medici brothers, did the conspiracy get under way. The assassination alone was not enough. To effect a revolution in Florence so that it would be delivered into Papal-Pazzi hands, there must be an armed force ready to threaten the city from the outside. Two sets of agents thus became necessary, one to organise the murders, the other to muster the levies to attack Florence as soon as it had been thrown into confusion.

The first co-operator was conveniently to hand in the person of Francesco Salviati, whom the Pope had nominated Archbishop of Pisa and who, for the last three years, had been refused entrance to his see by Lorenzo on the grounds that he had given a promise to the Pisans that there should be no appointment which had not been ratified by the *Signoria*. Lorenzo may also have been influenced by the fact that Salviati was, according to Poliziano, a man 'as gods and men well know', of infamous character, stained with every crime, sunk in every profligacy, a gambler and a sycophant, but bold, cunning and insolent.

For the organisation of the outside attack was chosen Giovanni Battista di

Opposite: *Anonymous portrait of Lorenzo the Magnificent.*

Montesecco, a *condottiere* in the Papal service, a man of good family who was by no means merely a professional cut-throat. Montesecco insisted on two things. Unless Jacopo de' Pazzi, as head of the house in Florence, was fully involved, the thing would be a failure. 'My Lords', he said, 'look to what you do, for Florence is a big affair.' The second point made by the *condottiere* was that he must have a personal assurance that the Pope approved of the plan in its entirety, including the murders of Lorenzo and Giuliano. Riario, the Archbishop Salviati and Francesco de' Pazzi thereupon arranged an audience for him at which Sixtus said: 'I do not desire the death of anyone since it is not in accord of Our office to consent to anyone's death. Though Lorenzo is a villain and behaves badly towards Us, We do not desire his death – only a change in the government of Florence.'

'But should it happen,' pressed Montesecco, 'would Your Holiness pardon him who did it?'

'You are a beast', ('*Tu sei una bestia*') said the Pope. 'I tell you I do not desire the death of anyone, but only a change of government. And I repeat, Gian Battista, that I desire very strongly that a change should take place in the government of Florence and that it should be removed from the hands of Lorenzo. From the moment he is out of Florence, We shall be able to do whatever We wish with that State and that will be very pleasing to Us.'

'Be content', said Archbishop Salviati, 'that we will do everything necessary to effect this end.'

'And you can be content', the Pope answered, 'that We will give you every assistance by way of men-at-arms or otherwise as you may consider necessary.'

The conspirators then left the Vatican and went to Florence to report the conversation to Jacopo de' Pazzi, who correctly interpreted it as meaning that Sixtus was prepared to support the conspiracy actively with troops, and would turn a blind eye to murder if murder were regrettably found to be necessary. His 'otherwise as you may consider necessary' was sufficient for the men to whom he was talking; and henceforward Jacopo became as energetic as he had hitherto been lethargic in his support of the plot.

The major difficulty which faced the conspirators was to find or to manufacture an occasion on which Lorenzo and Giuliano would be together and unarmed. To leave either alive after the death of the other would be to court disaster. Riario's first idea was to lure them to Rome under pretence of Lorenzo's discussing with the Pope the political and financial matters on which they disagreed. 'I have not the least doubt', he assured Lorenzo in the

Opposite: *Angelo Poliziano with Lorenzo's fifth child Giuliano de' Medici: detail from a fresco by Ghirlandaio.*

The blazon of the Pazzi family.

letter of invitation, 'that the Holy Father will receive you with joy while I, from the affection I feel for you, would behave so as fully to satisfy Your Magnificence, and all grievances which may have arisen will disappear.'

Certain that Lorenzo would fall into the trap, Riario informed Montesecco that the Medici brothers would visit Rome at Easter and would never return to Florence.

166

'Does His Holiness know of this?' asked the *condottiere*.

'Of course', Riario answered. 'Surely you realise that he will let us do whatever we wish. The only thing he requires is that it should turn out well.'

Lorenzo, however, did not accept the Papal invitation and the conspirators had to face the fact that the assassination would have to be accomplished in Florence. To facilitate this, Archbishop Salviati found an excuse to visit the city. The ruler of Faenza had become seriously ill and it was plausible enough that the possibilities in the event of his death should be thoroughly discussed by all the interested parties, which included Lorenzo and Salviati. Once safely inside the city, the Archbishop lost no time in organising the murder gang. The heads of the conspiracy in Florence were seven – Jacopo and Francesco de' Pazzi, the Archbishop himself with his brother and a Salviati cousin, a Humanist, Jacopo di Poggio Bracciolini, remarkable for his eloquence and his knowledge of history, who was beholden to the Medici for many favours but had squandered his patrimony and was deeply in debt, and Bernardo Bandini, a man who, like Poggio, had dissipated his fortune and had become an adventurer ready for any desperate enterprise to recover himself. In addition to the seven were now Montesecco himself, who had completed the plans for the external attack, and two priests, one of whom was a tutor in the Pazzi household and the other a Volterran who sought revenge for Lorenzo's treatment of his native city.

Everything was now ready except the occasion. Francesco Pazzi suggested that the best means of ensuring that Lorenzo and Giuliano should be present and off their guard would be to provide a banquet or some ecclesiastical celebration in honour of some distinguished person. Riario suggested that his seventeen-year-old nephew, Raffaelle Sansoni, who had recently been made a cardinal by his grandfather, the Pope, and had been studying at Lorenzo's new academy at Pisa, would be an ideal guest. The young Cardinal entered into the plan with enthusiasm and wrote to the unsuspecting Lorenzo letters of such charm that he was invited to visit the Medici villa at Fiesole.

On the occasion of the visit, however, Giuliano was taken ill at the last moment and unable to accompany his brother. The young Cardinal thereupon suggested that, as he was eager to see the Medici treasures, he should be invited to their palace on April 26. The day was the Sunday before Ascension Day and the whole company could then proceed to the Duomo where he could officially attend High Mass. Lorenzo agreed and preparations for a great banquet were made to which a distinguished company was invited including the ambassadors of Milan, Naples and Ferrara. Giuliano, however, still did not feel well enough for the banquet, though he promised to meet the guests at Mass in the cathedral.

The conspirators welcomed the alteration. It would be easier to carry out the murder at Mass, especially if they chose the moment of the Elevation of the Host, when, in reverence, the brothers would be bareheaded and on their knees.

Then an unexpected obstacle presented itself. Montesecco, to whom the killing of Lorenzo had been entrusted, flatly refused to do the deed at that time and in that place. As a soldier under orders he was prepared to kill Lorenzo at the banquet or in some neutral place. As a good Catholic, nothing would induce him to commit so monstrous a sacrilege as was now proposed. Riario and Pazzi had thus to rely on the two priests, who immediately offered their services. With the Archbishop and the Cardinal assuring them that the Pope had authorised the removal of the brothers, who were they to question ecclesiastical propriety?

Giuliano was to be dealt with by Francesco de' Pazzi and Bernardo Bandini; Archbishop Salviati with his brother, his cousin and Bracciolini were responsible for surrounding and capturing the palace of the *Signoria* and the great bell was to be rung to summon the citizens to hear Jacopo de' Pazzi proclaim that tyranny was dead; and Montesecco had charge of the mercenary forces which were to descend on the 'liberated' city.

On the Sunday morning, the young Cardinal presented himself with his train at the Medici palace where he was ceremonially welcomed and taken upstairs to a room prepared for him to change into his ecclesiastical vestments. This done, Lorenzo accompanied by Archbishop Salviati conducted him on the four-minute walk to the cathedral door. Here Salviati, who had other work to do, left them, and Lorenzo led the Cardinal to the chair prepared for him in choir (for the Cardinal, not being a priest, had no part to play at the altar). Lorenzo then returned to his own friends in the ambulatory.

As Mass was about to begin, the conspirators realised that Giuliano was absent. His two appointed murderers thereupon returned quickly to the Medici palace to fetch him. With a great show of affection they embraced him, putting their arms round him to feel whether he was by any chance wearing a mail shirt beneath his doublet. In their relief at finding that he was not, they joked that he had put on weight during his illness. On arriving at the cathedral, Giuliano, accompanied by one servant, but with the assassination gang pressing close behind him in the crowded congregation, took up his position on the southern side of the ambulatory, near the chapel of the Holy Cross, separated from Lorenzo by the full width of the choir.

At the signal agreed upon, the sound of the sanctus bell announcing the Elevation, Bandini drove his dagger into Giuliano's side and Francesco de' Pazzi brought his sword down with full force on to his bare head. He fell dead immediately and the lesser Pazzi adherents crowded round to add their dagger-thrusts. The body had nineteen wounds.

Anonymous sixteenth-century drawing of the façade of the Cathedral in Florence,
where Giuliano de' Medici was murdered.

misaunum : quia ego
dixi uobis. In uig-
lia pent. fm iohanne.
Illo tempore. t
Dixit iesus disci
pulis suis. Si diligitis
me : mandata mea s-
uate. Et ego rogabo
patrem et alium para
clitum dabit uobis a-
ut maneat uobiscum
in etinum spiritum uei-
tatis : que mundus o
non potest accipere : qa
non uidet eum nec scit
eum. Vos autem cog-
scetis eum : quia apud
uos manebit : et inno-
bis erit. Non relinqu..
uos orphanos : ueniaa
ad uos. Adhuc modi
cum : et mundus iam
non uidet. Vos aute
uidetis me : quia ego
uino : et uos uiuetis.

In illo die uos cogno
scetis quia ego sum in
patre meo : et uos in me:
et ego in uobis. Qui
habet mandata mea t
seruat ea : ille est qui t
diligit me. Qui aute
diligit me : diligetur
a patre meo. et ego di
ligam eum : et manife
stabo ei meipsum : ~

In die pent. fm iohez

Illo tem
pore. Di
xit iesus
discipulis
suis. Si
quis dili
git me : sermonem me
um seruabit. Et pater
meus diliget eum : et
ad eum ueniemus : et
mansionem apud eu-
faciemus. Qui non di
ligit me : sermones t

On the other side of the choir, the two priests were less successful. At the sound of the sanctus bell, the Volterran priest, Maffei, raised his dagger and to steady himself for the mortal blow, put his left hand on Lorenzo's shoulder. Instantly turning round, Lorenzo saw the raised dagger and instinctively wound his mantle round his left arm as he raised it to ward off the blow which, so deflected, inflicted only a flesh wound on his neck. Drawing his sword, he leapt over the wooden screen dividing the ambulatory from the choir and made for the door of the new sacristy behind the High Altar. Bandini and Francesco de' Pazzi, seeing him, realised that the priests' attempt had failed and, with their followers, left the corpse of Giuliano and rushed into the choir to intercept him before he could reach the safety of the sacristy. By this time, however, a body of Lorenzo's faithful friends, led by Poliziano, had rallied round him. Two of them, at great peril to themselves counter-attacked the murder gang and, though one was killed and the other wounded, gave Lorenzo time to reach the sacristy and Poliziano and the others to slam the brazen gates in the face of the assassins.

While these deeds were being done in the Duomo, Archbishop Salviati, with the thirty men allotted to him and about twenty Perugian desperadoes who had been imported into Florence to support the plot made his way to the palace of the *Signoria* and sent a message to the Gonfalonier that he had come with special news from the Pope. The Gonfalonier, who was at dinner, gave orders that he should be admitted to the reception-room to wait while his followers were put into various other small rooms, so that they were, in Poliziano's phrase, 'split up into several small rivulets'.

When the Gonfalonier eventually received the Archbishop to hear the pretended message from the Pope, he found Salviati so incoherent from excitement and uncertainty that he immediately became suspicious and called the guard. Salviati rushed from the room calling to his followers in the various rooms that the moment had come. But the only answer was cries of rage and a beating on the walls. They were all locked in. It was the custom for each succeeding Gonfalonier to change all locks as a precaution against treachery. The present one had showed particular ingenuity in having the doors made so that they closed and bolted on the slightest impulse and could not be opened from the inside except by those acquainted with the complicated mechanism.

Meanwhile Lorenzo and his friends safe in the new sacristy at the Duomo, knew nothing but the simple fact that they were safe. A fifteen-year-old boy, Arnoldo Ridolfi, who was passionately fond of Lorenzo, insisted on sucking

Opposite: *A page from the Gospels which lay open on the High Altar at the moment when Giuliano was murdered.*

Botticelli's portrait of Giuliano de' Medici, Lorenzo's brother: compare with the anonymous bust opposite.

the wound in his neck, lest the priest's dagger had been poisoned, while another, Stefano della Stufa, ran up the ladders leading to the organ-loft where from a window he could look down into the cathedral. The first thing he saw was the mutilated body of Giuliano, lying where it had fallen. But this he did not report to Lorenzo. Having satisfied himself that the church was in the hands of friends, he announced that it was safe to leave. The sacristy doors were opened and Lorenzo with Poliziano at his side and protected by a moving square of supporters was conducted to his home, great care being taken that he had no opportunity to see his brother's body.

An immense crowd immediately assembled outside the Medici palace, intent on assuring itself that he was safe. It seemed that every man in Florence, from the youngest to the oldest, had snatched up arms to defend the Medici. Lorenzo came out on the balcony, his neck bandaged, and addressed them, imploring them to moderate the violence of their just resentment of the

Anonymous bust of Giuliano de' Medici, who was murdered by the Pazzi conspirators in 1478.

Pazzi and leave to the magistrates the task of finding and punishing the guilty lest the innocent should be wrongfully destroyed. He felt more anxiety, at the moment, from the intemperate anxiety of his well-wishers than he had from the hatred of his enemies. At this moment of retribution, the honour of Florence must not be tarnished.

Moderation, however, once Giuliano's death was known, was a vain hope. The citizens became a vengeance-seeking mob. The Pazzi adherents, the followers of Salviati, the Perugians were cut down where they stood; heads stuck on lances were soon being carried about the city. The Pazzi palace was sacked and the naked body of Francesco, who was hiding there, dragged through the streets to the palace of the *Signoria* to suffer the summary justice of being thrown alive from one of the upper windows for the mob on the piazza below to tear apart – a fate shared by Archbishop Salviati's two relatives. The Archbishop himself was hanged in his episcopal robes and

173

suspended from a window, his body dangling against the wall at a height just above the heads of the people.

The two priests had taken refuge in the Benedictine abbey and remained in safety for two days, but as soon as their hiding-place became known the mob surrounded the abbey and threatened to kill all the monks unless the criminals were surrendered. They were surrendered and hanged. Jacopo de' Pazzi managed to escape into the open country, but in the village of Castagno he was recognised and sent back to Florence where he was hanged. Montesecco was not captured until May 1. He was brought to trial and made a full confession of all the circumstances, including the part played by the Pope and Girolamo Riario. The *condottiere* was beheaded in the courtyard of the *Podestà's* palace on May 4. But the young Cardinal was spared, partly because of his youth, partly because the evidence pointed to the fact that he had been basically ignorant of the conspiracy and used as a catspaw by his uncle, Girolamo.

Bandini, who had struck the first blow at Giuliano managed to escape to Constantinople where he imagined he would be safe, but the Sultan, at Lorenzo's request, had him arrested and sent back in chains to Florence to face trial and death – an action which, more than anything else, impressed Florence with a sense of Lorenzo's power and position in the world.

On the Thursday, Ascension Day, Giuliano was given a magnificent funeral in San Lorenzo. The Florentines, who were accustomed to devote that particular feast to going out into the fields to greet the spring and catch grasshoppers, attended it in force and the young men who had been his friends and companions wore mourning garments as they pressed round the grave with genuine and unaffected grief.

As an expression of their gratitude that Lorenzo himself had escaped, the *Signoria* commissioned three life-size figures of him to be modelled in wax under the superintendence of Verrocchio. One, representing him as he appeared on the balcony with his neck bandaged, was placed in the convent of Augustinian nuns in the Via san Gallo, which was particularly under Medici patronage. The second, showing Lorenzo in the dress of an ordinary citizen, was given to the Church of the Annunciation, the mother church of the Servite Order which contained a miraculous image of Our Lady and, as one of the most celebrated shrines of Italy already contained two hundred or so wax effigies of visiting celebrities, donated by themselves. They were hung from the rafters of the nave, but Lorenzo was given a place to himself 'over the

Opposite: *Sketch by Leonardo da Vinci of the hanging on December 28, 1478 of Bernardo Bandini, the Pazzi conspirator who actually murdered Giuliano de' Medici.*

small door where the wax lights are sold'. The third was sent to the Church of St Mary of the Angels at Assisi.

The *Signoria*, not content with this special commemoration of Lorenzo, decided to perpetuate the memory of the event itself by commissioning Botticelli, for a fee of forty florins, to paint upon the façade of the palazzo a representation of the punishment of the conspirators. According to Vasari, the work was so realistic that the passer-by could imagine that he still saw the bodies themselves dangling from the windows. Those represented were three Pazzi, three Salviati (the Archbishop in his vestments) Bernardo Bandini, hanging by his neck, and Francesco, a friend of Lorenzo's Pazzi brother-in-law who, according to Poliziano, was wrongly arrested and in any case was not proceeded against, hanging by his foot. To each Lorenzo appended a suitable epitaph. Under the portrait of Bandini whom as Giuliano's murderer, he most hated, he wrote:

> *Son Bernardo Bandini, un nuovo Giuda*
> *Traditore micidiale a chiesa io fui.*
> *Ribello per aspettare morte più cruda*

'I am Bernardo Bandini, another Judas. A murderous traitor in a church was I. A rebel doomed to await death even harder'.

As regards the Pazzi, the *Signoria* decreed that the very name of the family should be blotted out. It was an offence even to pronounce it; whoever should marry into it was thereby excluded from any public office and wherever its coat of arms was found it was to be erased. All its property was confiscated. Socially and politically it was utterly crushed.

From this moment Lorenzo was left to rule Florence almost as he would, the absolute and unquestioned lord of the city and the hearts of its people.

Commemorative medal of the Pazzi conspiracy: on the recto *Lorenzo who escaped death,* on the verso *Giuliano who did not.*

War of Words

When the news of the failure of the conspiracy arrived in Rome, the Pope and his son were beside themselves with fury. Girolamo Riario immediately took three hundred halberdiers to arrest the Florentine ambassador, Acciaiuoli, who was then hauled through the streets vehemently protesting at this breach of protocol. The Pope was on the point of committing him to prison in San Angelo when the Venetian and the Milanese ambassadors protested that, if he took such a course, they would accompany their colleague to prison. Acciaiuoli was consequently released; but, instead, the Holy Father ordered the arrest of all the Florentines living in Rome and prepared to excommunicate Lorenzo and put Florence and its dependencies under an Interdict. Their crime was that they had hanged Archbishop Salviati.

The excommunication (which Roscoe quaintly called 'one of the most extraordinary specimens of priestly arrogance which has ever insulted the common sense of mankind') described Lorenzo as 'that son of iniquity and foster-child of perdition, with a heart harder than Pharaoh's' who, with his accomplices 'kindled with madness, torn by diabolical suggestions and led like dogs to savage madness, disgracefully raged against ecclesiastical persons and laid violent hands upon the Archbishop, detained him prisoner for several hours and hanged him on a Sunday from the windows of the Palazzo.'

Consequently, 'Lorenzo, the *Priori*, the Gonfalonier, the Eight, are pronounced to be culpable, sacrilegious, excommunicate, anathematised, infamous, unworthy of trust and incapable of making a will. All their property was to be surrendered to the Church, their houses were to be levelled to the ground so that their habitations would be desolate and that none might ever thereafter dwell therein. Let everlasting ruin witness their everlasting shame!'

Interdict was also pronounced against the city itself, unless by July 1 it had brought the offenders to justice. Florence was to be stripped of its archiespiscopal rank and pontifical dignities. Mass could not be said; no one could be baptised or shriven or buried; all festivities which were immemorially

177

associated with St John the Baptist's Day (June 24) were immediately to be cancelled.

On June 10 Florence appointed the Ten of War, of whom Lorenzo was one, to muster forces in case of war and the *Signoria* composed a 'Brief Answer' in which, with biting irony it replied: 'Your Holiness says you are only waging war against our State to free it from a tyrant. We are grateful for your paternal love, but we cannot without sorrow behold an army of the Shepherd entering our territories (when the enemy of all Christendom, the Turk himself, is on the threshold of Italy), ravaging its crops, seizing its villages and carrying off its maidens and the treasures of its shrines as booty.' They added that now they were assured that these actions sprang from the Pope's love, and not his hatred, they were emboldened to ask that the exile of Lorenzo should be shown to be for the advantages of the Republic.

Meanwhile the Interdict was treated as of no effect and the clergy were ordered to perform their functions as usual. St John the Baptist's Day was observed, a week late it is true, but with all, if not more than, its traditional splendours. And Gentile, Bishop of Arezzo, Lorenzo's first tutor, summoned a special meeting of the clergy of Florence in which they publicly incriminated the Pope as the real instigator of the Pazzi conspiracy and the consequent enormities committed in the city. To the Papal accusation that Lorenzo was a tyrant, they answered: 'We and the people have proved him to be, and with one voice we acclaim that he is, the defender of our liberties. We are prepared to sacrifice everything for his safety, which is the one undoubted guarantee of the safety and liberty of the State. Your charges move us to laughter, for you wish us to drive out a man who has in no way degenerated from his illustrious forebears, Cosmo and Piero; a man to whom no one in Florence is to be preferred for true religion, worship of God, charity and piety.'

Perhaps, the document continued, the true grounds of the Pope's anger, could have been expressed in very different terms. 'Had he permitted himself to be slaughtered by your atrocious satellites whom you sent to Florence for that purpose; had we failed to recover our Palazzo Publico, the citadel of our liberties, from the hands of your traitors; had we delivered up ourselves, our magistrates and our citizens to you to be assassinated, then there would be no cause of contention between us!'

And who is the true enemy of the Christian Faith? 'Since you have occupied the Chair of Peter, everyone knows how you have used your office. It is too well known who is the enemy of the public good. Put on, then, a better mind. Remember that the Keys were not given you for such uses. Indeed we fear that in our time that saying of the Gospel will be fulfilled: "He will miserably destroy the wicked, and his vineyard shall another take." '

The letter ended with the declaration that Florence 'will resolutely

Ghirlandaio's portrait of Gentile Becchi, Bishop of Arezzo, who had been Lorenzo's first tutor.

defend her liberties, trusting in Christ, who knows the justice of her cause; trusting in her allies, who regard her cause as their own; trusting especially in the Most Christian King, Louis of France, who has always been the Patron and Protector of the Florentine State.'

The sting was in the tail. Referring to the French lilies which the Medici officially bore on their arms, Louis replied that his own honour was at stake as much as that of Florence and that the murder of Giuliano, 'his cousin', was tantamount to an attempt on his own person. The King sent Philippe de Commines as a special ambassador, with a guard of six hundred men, to support Lorenzo and to threaten the Pope that France would withdraw its allegiance to him and would appeal to a General Council of the Church (the bugbear of the Papacy for generations) unless the censures against Florence were revoked and the conspirators punished.

On July 25 Commines was in Florence, where fifty-five pounds' weight of

179

silver plate from the *Signoria* and three hundred jewels from Lorenzo himself betokened the gratitude of the Republic.

But whether or not Louis of France was willing to make war on the Pope in Lorenzo's interest (and no one seriously expected it) there was little doubt that Lorenzo would refuse to allow it. According to his friend and first biographer, Niccolo Valori, Lorenzo proclaimed unequivocally: 'A united Italy could successfully oppose any attempt upon her from beyond the Alps, but were she divided against herself she could not endure, but would fall a ready victim to the aggression of an ultramontane power. For this reason he refused, in his war with the Pope, to call in the assistance of the King of France, declaring that there was nothing on earth which could justify the adoption of methods which, while securing his personal safety, might lead to the ruin of Italy. Far better would it be to pray to God that it would never enter the head of the King of France to try an experiment with his forces in Italy, since against such an attempt, there could be no remedy.'

Lorenzo preferred to allow the Chancellor of the *Signoria* to epitomise the case against the Pope in a document, temperately but conclusively written, which could be circulated to the rulers of Europe. Essentially it was a brief narrative of what actually happened in Florence on that fatal April 26. The Chancellor included Montesecco's confession, which put the Pope's guilt beyond contradiction. He pointed out that the troops sent to engineer the revolution were mercenaries in Sixtus's pay. 'And now', he continued indignantly, 'we are put under interdict and separated from the communion of the Faithful. What treachery could not accomplish is now to be achieved by ecclesiastical censures and force of arms. War is to be carried on against us by Sixtus, Pontifex Maximus, and other illustrious persons who guide the rudder of the Church, for no other reason than that we have not allowed ourselves to be slaughtered and that we have defended our Palazzo, our city and our liberties. Thus a mighty army, in the service of the High Priest of all Christians, swoops down upon a most religious people. In us, unless we deceive ourselves, the whole cause of Christendom is at stake, for as long as Sixtus carries on his wars, it is beset with manifest peril, while those open and most powerful enemies, the Turks, insolently rage upon the threshold of Italy.'

The Pope felt it incumbent on him to discount as far as possible the effect on other nations of the Florentine revelations of his part in the conspiracy. He wrote to his Captain-General, the Duke of Urbino, commenting on the charges made in the letter of the *Signoria* and saying that he can only imagine

Opposite: *Portrait of Louis XI, King of France, attributed to Colin d'Amiens.*

Messire Phelippe de Comines ss dangenton
historien

that God has deprived the writers of their reason as punishment for their wickedness. As for himself, all his intentions are just and right and all his hopes are in God, for it is His honour and His glory which are at stake. He himself, Sixtus, has no quarrel with anyone but that ungrateful, heretic, excommunicate son of iniquity, Lorenzo de' Medici. The Pope ended his missive by suggesting that Urbino, who was a Knight of the Garter and had some influence with King Edward IV of England, should write to that monarch putting things in their true perspective.

It is not known whether the Duke obliged in that matter, but there remains extant a letter from him to Milan trying to detach her from the Triple Alliance by suggesting that Lorenzo, in opposing the Pope, 'had sinned against the Holy Ghost'.

Milan, however, remained true to her engagements. The weak link, as far as Lorenzo was concerned, was Ferrante of Naples. In his case no one, not even Lorenzo, supposed that long-standing friendship would outweigh self-interest, or that a man of Ferrante's character, whatever sentiments he might think it wise publicly to express, would have been shocked if Sixtus had taken part in the murder of Giuliano with his own hand. The matter, as far as Ferrante was concerned, reduced itself to one of personal and political aggrandisement, and it took him a very short time to decide that it would be easier for him to realise his own ambitions in Tuscany if Lorenzo were out of the way and that he was likely to gain more for himself by supporting the Pope than by opposing him. If he allied himself with the Papal States and Siena, he foresaw a reasonable chance of being able to use Sienese territory as a base for operations against Florence and Tuscany, which might result in the re-establishments of the old Neapolitan overlordship of that region, while an alliance with Lorenzo, involving the adhesion of Naples to the Northern League, would immediately invalidate schemes of hegemony.

In little more than a month after Giuliano's murder, Ferrante's son, the Duke of Calabria (Lorenzo's friend and correspondent) was in Rome conveying to the Pope assurances of his father's goodwill and discussing a plan of campaign.

By September, the Neapolitan forces, led by the Duke of Calabria, actually crossed the frontier of Florence and were encamped a little to the south of Montepulciano, while Urbino, in command of the Papal troops, was also named generalissimo of the combined forces. The generalissimo of the Florentine forces was Ercole d'Este, Duke of Ferrara, who happened to be the brother-in-law of his opponent, the Duke of Calabria (and thus

Opposite: *Portrait of Philippe de Commines, Louis XI's special ambassador to Florence: from the* Recueil d'Arras.

Portrait by Pedro Berruguete of Federigo da Montefeltro, Duke of Urbino, who may have preferred his books to his job as Captain-General of the Florentine armed forces.

son-in-law of Ferrante). As both sides adhered to the *condottiere* principle of avoiding pitched battles, the desultory nature of the conflict was increased; and as the astrological consultation of the stars foretold that their conjunctions would not prove propitious to Florence until September 27, d'Este had some excuse for his natural apathy. In spite of much marching and counter-marching and occasional skirmishes, the autumn campaign showed nothing of importance but the fall of San Sevino to the Papalists, after a long and pointless negotiation, after which, in the November of 1498, both sides retired thankfully into their winter quarters.

The Crisis of His Fate

As soon as the actual fighting ceased, the King of France made increased efforts to bring about a diplomatic victory for Florence. Quite apart from his admiration for Lorenzo's ability, Louis XI, in his middle-fifties and, having created the first standing army known to Christendom, the strongest monarch in Europe, saw himself in a quasi-paternal rôle. In this he was confirmed by Philippe de Commines's report to him from Florence: 'The Florentines might consider it good fortune that they were not defeated on all sides for, as it was long since they had been engaged in war, they could not measure the danger they were in. Lorenzo de' Medici who guides affairs in the city is young and influenced by the younger generation. His opinion is held in high estimation.' And Lorenzo himself wrote to Louis: 'Today, as always, I think I shall need the assistance, favour and protection of Your Majesty, to whom I shall turn in confidence for all that concerns me, as to my true lord, protector and patron, my help and my refuge.'

In the November of 1478 Louis sent a special embassy to the Pope to impress on him the imperative necessity of the union of Christendom against the Turks. Such combined action was impossible as long as Sixtus himself was the storm-centre of Italy. Let him abandon the war and call an Ecumenical Council which could summon all Christian countries to unite against the common foe. The questions in dispute between the Pope and Lorenzo de' Medici should be submitted to arbitration and thoroughly examined so that Lorenzo's case was properly understood. At any rate, let active hostilities remain suspended under a flag of truce until the French proposals had been reasonably considered.

In the January of 1479, the furious Pope replied, denying Louis's right to intervene, refusing to call an Ecumenical Council, reiterating his complaints against Lorenzo and insisting that he should confess his guilt and be suitably punished for his sacrilegious violence to ecclesiastical personages. Nevertheless, Louis's example inspired other protests. An embassy from King

Edward IV of England, reinforcing the French demands, arrived in Rome in the early spring. Ambassadors from Venice and Milan supported the calling of a Council if France would, over the Pope's head, summon one at Lyons.

The Pope, in the circumstances, thought it prudent to gain time and, in April, suspended the Interdict on Florence while the whole matter was referred to a Commission of Cardinals.

The Commission drew up careful terms intended to be rejected. The question of the provocation given by the Pazzi conspiracy was entirely ignored. Florence must acknowledge her sins and make atonement; Botticelli's pictures on the wall of the Palazzo must be erased; Florentine fortresses on the border of the Romagna were to be surrendered to the Pope, who must also be compensated for all the expenses of the war and given a solemn assurance that Florence would never again make war on the Holy See.

Obviously peace was, and on the Pope's side was meant to be, impossible. At the end of April hostilities were resumed between the armies in the Chiana valley to the south-west of Florence, in which the Florentine objective was to fight a defensive action in such a way as to protect themselves against the approach of the enemy to the city itself.

The Neapolitan troops found Siena, the age-long rival of Florence, accommodating as a basis of attack up the river valleys and, operating in the Elsa valley, won the most important action of the war at Poggio Imperiale whose fall left the way to Florence unguarded. Instead of advancing on the city, however, the Neapolitans decided to secure their rear by taking the little fortified town of Colle. But Colle put up a gallant resistance for two months, by which time the Neapolitans had lost any advantage they might have gained and were only too glad to declare a truce and retire to Siena. In gratitude to the rulers of Colle, Lorenzo proposed that the citizenship of Florence should be bestowed on them. He himself was particularly grateful for the time gained for diplomatic manoeuvre, for, in spite of a success when the Papalist army was defeated in the neighbourhood of the ill-omened Thrasymene Lake (where Hannibal had overcome the Romans), Lorenzo realised that Florence could not face another campaign. The Republic's resources had been strained to the limit; new taxes could hardly be levied on the increasingly unwilling citizens; the *condottieri*, intent only on booty, quarrelled among themselves and had to be kept apart from each other as far as possible; outbreaks of the plague, though mercifully comparatively light at the moment, menaced the future. Most disturbing of all were the signs of panic which the Florentines had shown at the approach of the

Opposite: *Louis XI of France with his Knights of the Order of St Michael: anonymous.*

Neapolitan army before it turned aside to reduce Colle. And the truce after Colle gave an opportunity to some of the older citizens publicly to express their opinion that enough blood had been shed and that it would be more becoming for Lorenzo to negotiate a peace to follow the truce rather than concern himself with preparing a third campaign of a ruinous war.

By one of the curious coincidences of history the day which saw the Florentine defeat at Poggio Imperiale – September 7, 1479 – saw also the return to power in Milan of the boy-Duke's uncle, Ludovico Sforza, called 'The Moor'. This meant that Milan, weak and distracted since the murder of Ludovico's elder brother on that St Stephen's Day of 1476, could once more fulfil its original rôle in the Triple Alliance. Lorenzo immediately wrote to Ludovico welcoming him back and pointing out that the old and tried friendship was as necessary to Milan as to Florence. If any Italian power were allowed to aggrandise itself at the expense of Florence, Milan would feel the effect which could not fail to be disastrous.

Ludovico replied that he could not, unfortunately, be of material assistance to Lorenzo, but that he would willingly use his influence with Ferrante of Naples (his sister, Hippolita, had married Ferrante's son) to restore the alliance in full. Let Lorenzo come to terms with Ferrante who, he was sure, would reject no reasonable terms. '*Inter os et offam multa accidere possent. Jactet aleam!*' (Twixt cup and lip much may happen. Let him make a throw!)

Another external event which influenced the situation was the growing menace of the Turks who, under the great Mohammed II, called 'The Conqueror', had raided the very outskirts of Venice and were demanding an annual tribute of ten thousand ducats for permission to trade in the Black Sea.

Reflecting on these matters, Lorenzo decided on a course of action which, perhaps, none but he could have dared to take. At the outset of the war, he had sent his wife and children out of the city for safety against siege. Now he would deliver himself into the hands of Ferrante, trusting that the long years of family friendship would, at a personal confrontation, obliterate the recent enmity. On November 24 he sent a message to the effect that he would willingly agree to whatever Ferrante should think best for the unification of the Italian States, provided that peace was made and captured Florentine

Opposite: The siege of Colle: painting by Gabelle in 1479. By resisting the assaults of the Neapolitan troops, the small town of Colle in the Elsa valley gave Lorenzo valuable time for diplomatic negotiations: in gratitude, he proposed that citizenship of Florence should be bestowed upon the leaders of Colle.

COLLE DI VALDELSA

QVESTA · E L ENTRATA · E L VSCITA · DELLA · GENEBALE · KABELLA · DELCHO
MVNO · DISIENA · ALTEMPO · DESAVI · HVOMINI · FRANCIESCHO · DIT
O MASSO · DILVTOCCO · ⚜ · E FRANCIESCHO · DE ROCHI · E · FRACESCHO ·
DI · FILIPPO · DIĀ · LOREŌ · E DOMENICHO · DELVECHIO · E BARTALOME
O · DI BIDINO · SARAGINI · QVATRO · MAESTRI · P SEI · MESI · E · DI · MŜ ·
FORESE · DI · NANI · DISTEFANO · E · DOMENICHO · DI · MISERE · LOREŌ
DE ROCHI · E · NICHOLO · SER · GARDI · E MVCATTO · CERCEANI · ALTRE · QVATRO ·
MAESTRI · CHOMICANDO · IIDETTO · VFFITIO · ADDI · PRIMO · DIGENAIO · ＡＣＣＣＣＬＸＸＶ
III E FINITO · ADDI · VITIMO · DIDICEBRE · ＡＣＣＣＣＬＸＸＶIIII · E GIOVANI · DIFRANCIESC
HIO GABRIELLI · SCRITTORE

towns restored. A week later he privately entrusted the government to the tried and trusted Tommaso Soderini and secretly set out for Pisa, whence he intended to embark for Naples.

On December 7, from San Miniato, he wrote to the *Signoria* a letter of explanation so characteristic of him that it must be given in full: 'If I did not explain to you, before I left Florence, the cause of my departure, it was not from want of respect but because I thought that, in the dangerous circumstances in which our city is placed, it was more necessary to act than to deliberate. It seems to me that peace has become essential to us; and as all other means of attaining it have proved ineffective I have chosen to incur some degree of danger to myself rather than to allow the Republic to continue any longer under its present difficulties. I therefore intend, with your permission, to go direct to Naples, hoping that, as I am the person chiefly aimed at by our enemies, I may by delivering myself into their hands perhaps be the means of restoring peace to my fellow-citizens.

'Of these alternatives, one must be taken for granted. Either the King of Naples – as he has often asserted and as some have believed – is friendly to the Republic of Florence and intends even in hostility rather to render us a service than to deprive us of our liberties: or he wishes to effect our ruin. If the first be true and he is favourably disposed towards us, there is no better way of putting his intention to the test than by placing myself freely in his hands – and indeed I venture to say that this is the only means of obtaining an honourable peace. If, on the other hand, the real attitude of the King extends to the subversion of our liberties, we shall at least be speedily apprised of his intentions; and this knowledge will be more cheaply obtained by the ruin of one than of all.

'I am content to take this risk upon myself because as I am the person principally sought after, I shall be a better test of the King's intentions, for it is possible that my destruction is all that is aimed at; also, as I have had more honour and consideration among you than my merits deserve and perhaps more than have in our days been bestowed on any private citizen, I consider myself more particularly bound than any other person to promote the interests of my country even to the sacrifice of my life.

'With this full intention I now go; and it may be the will of God that, as this war was begun in the blood of my brother so it may be by my blood concluded. All that I desire is that my life and my death, my prosperity and

Opposite: *Botticelli painted* Pallas and the Centaur *to memorialise the Florentine triumph over the Pope's devious behaviour: the Centaur, symbolizing the Pazzi conspiracy, cowers before the Goddess of Wisdom, symbolizing Lorenzo and Florence, who is pulling him away from the crumbling Vatican.*

Left: *Lorenzo de' Medici (Florence) : detail of a fresco by Ottavio Vannini.*
Right: *Don Ferrante (Naples) : anonymous engraving.*

my misfortunes, may contribute towards the welfare of my native place. Should the result conform to my wishes, I shall rejoice at having obtained peace for my country and security for myself. Should it prove otherwise, my misfortunes will be alleviated by the knowledge that they were necessary for my country's welfare; for if our adversaries aim only at my destruction, I shall be in their power; and if their intentions range further, they will then be fully understood. In that case, I have no doubt that all my fellow-citizens will unite in defending their liberties to the last extremity and I trust with the same success as, by the favour of God, our ancestors have been able to do.

'These are the sentiments with which I shall make my journey, entreating God that I may be enabled to perform on this occasion what every citizen ought at all times to be ready to do for his country.'

When the letter was read to the *Signoria* there was general consternation. According to one account, most of the members unashamedly gave way to tears. Be that as it may, they rallied to Lorenzo in the most practical manner possible and instructed the Chancellor to write a letter, appointing him a special ambassador with full credentials to negotiate peace. This official status might at least protect him from the fate of the Milanese, Piccanini, who, with more claims to Ferrante's favour than Lorenzo had had, on a visit under safe-conduct to Naples, in defiance of all laws of honour and hospitality, been thrown into a dungeon and soon afterwards secretly murdered.

The letter of authorisation arrived while Lorenzo was at Pisa. On the evening of December 10, a Neapolitan galley anchored at the little port of Vada

Left: *Mahommed II (Constantinople): ascribed to Gentile Bellini*. Right: *Ludovico 'Il Moro' Sforza (Milan): portrait by Boltraffio*.

in the Pisan Maremma and next day Lorenzo went aboard, 'praying God' as he put it, 'that I may journey to Naples and back in safety and my purpose be attained'. On the afternoon of Saturday, December 18, he landed in Naples, where Ferrante's son and grandson were on the quay to welcome him and a great crowd had gathered to see the man whose name was on everybody's tongue. With great acclamation he was conducted to the palace opposite the Castelnuovo, Ferrante's own residence, which the King had apportioned to him.

His reception, indeed, was so favourable that the Venetians were suspicious and openly declared that the whole affair had been arranged beforehand by Ferrante and Lorenzo and that the appearance of an improvisation was only a blind to conceal a secret agreement already concluded. This was, of course, untrue, but as soon as the two men met face to face Lorenzo exerted on Ferrante the fascination which had existed from the first meeting in his boyhood. His arguments, too, were cogent enough. In a masterly sketch, he set before the King the essential politics of Italy, stressing the precariousness of Ludovico Sforza's position in Milan as long as his nephew the boy-Duke lived; the unreliability of Venice, forced by the Turks to concentrate on her own affairs; the worthlessness of Papal support, since Vatican policy changed with every new occupant of the Chair; so that the only secure friendship for Naples was Florence.

Lorenzo resided in Naples *en grand seigneur*, identifying himself as far as he could with the local nobility. He was boundlessly generous (as, fortunately, he could afford to be), sparing no expense, now in entertaining the nobility at banquets, now at dowering poor girls from the provinces, now at purchasing the freedom of galley-slaves and providing them with new clothes. His first biographer, Valori, says he remembers hearing what amount Lorenzo actually spent while he was in Naples, but that he does not dare to write it.

Within two months Lorenzo reaped his reward. In spite of every form of opposition and interference by the Pope, the rough draft of a treaty between Florence and Naples had been drawn up and agreed by the end of February. When Ferrante presented him with a magnificent horse, the peer of the one he had given him for the famous tournament twelve years before, Lorenzo, in thanking him, remarked that he who was the bearer of good news had need of so swift a steed. By mid-March he was back in Florence.

Valori has thus recorded his home-coming: 'He landed in Livorno, whence he went to Pisa. In the harbour and town he was received with such a manifestation of joy, with such signs of attachment and shouts of applause from the whole population that the place itself seemed to join in with the rejoicing. But it is impossible to describe how he was received at his entry into Florence. Young and old, men and women, all flocked together to him. The people and the nobles vied with each other in their rejoicing at his safe return. To all he gave his hand kindly and gratefully. The people embraced each other for joy.'

On the Feast of the Annunciation, March 25, the peace and alliance with Naples were formally proclaimed throughout Florence and the grandest of

Anonymous fifteenth-century painting of Naples.

processions, headed by the miraculous statue of Our Lady, went about the city.

The Pope, however, more furious than even, refused any *détente* until at the end of July seven thousand Turks landed in Apulia, laid siege to Otranto and captured it. In hardly more than a week after this irruption of reality, Sixtus had no alternative but to forgo his rage in return for whatever formal apology Florence cared to give. An embassy of twelve Florentine citizens was despatched to Rome, though Lorenzo was not among them as Sixtus had originally stipulated. They admitted that the Republic in the past had committed many errors of judgment, both public and private, of which the Pope, because of his divine nature, had better knowledge than even the Republic itself could possess. Nothing specific was mentioned. All was left vague, even ironical. There was no word about the causes of the quarrel; there was merely an expression of sorrow for errors, accompanied by the hope that in future the Holy See would be the friend and protector of Florence.

On December 3, the first Sunday of Advent 1480, in the portico of St Peter's, before the closed bronze gates of the central nave of the basilica, seated on a throne covered with purple silk, sat the Pope to receive the Florentine embassy. The noise made by the crowd of spectators rendered any oration inaudible, but the ritual gestures made the proceedings comprehensible enough – the humble kissing of Sixtus's toe by the Florentines, the Pope's touching each ambassador with a penitent's staff, followed by the Papal blessing and the throwing open of the gates so that the whole company could accompany the Holy Father to the High Altar for the celebration of Mass.

As for Lorenzo, Machiavelli summed the matter up with 'All men praised him extravagantly, declaring that by his prudence he had recovered in peace all that adverse fortune had taken from the Florentines in war and that by his discretion and judgment he had done more than the enemy with all the force of arms they could command.'

He was thirty, and for the remaining twelve years of his life he enjoyed an unquestioned supremacy. Florence voluntarily surrendered all power into the hands of one who, at a crisis, had been willing to surrender everything for her.

Botticelli memorialised the event in a masterpiece which is more un-intelligible than usual without a knowledge of events – *Pallas and the Centaur*. The Centaur, symbolising crime and war, typifies the iniquitous Pazzi conspiracy and the unrighteous war brought on Florence as a result of it. He cowers before the Goddess of Wisdom who, with Lorenzo's private crest of interlaced diamond rings covering her dress and wreathed with laurel further to emphasise the identification, pulls him gently by the hair away from the imposing, but crumbling, Vatican masonry. In the background is the Bay of Naples with a single ship riding at anchor.

Lorenzo himself summed up the crisis of his fate with his usual terseness: 'I shall only say that my sufferings have been very severe, the authors of them having been men of great authority and talents and fully determined to accomplish, by every means in their power, my total ruin. I, having nothing to oppose these formidable enemies but youth and inexperience (saving, indeed, the assistance I received from God's goodness) was reduced to such an extreme of misfortune that I had at one and the same time to labour under the excommunication of my soul and the dispersion of my property, to contend with endeavours to divest me of my authority in the State, to meet attempts to introduce discord into my family and to weather frequent plots to deprive me of my life; insomuch that I should at one time have thought death itself a lesser evil than those with which I had to contend.'

'Only a Citizen of Florence'

One thing inescapably clear to Lorenzo once he found himself in an unassailable position in a Republic at peace was the necessity to revise the Florentine constitution. The complicated structure of government, though possibly just adequate in its mania for democracy for internal administration, was totally useless in a situation requiring military action and diplomatic acumen. The short tenure of office by everyone concerned in it meant ultimately that no long-term decision could be taken in the name of the Republic. The delegated magistrates, conscious above everything of the limitation of their powers both in extent and in time would only reluctantly determine on and cautiously engage in courses of action which involved the welfare and possibly the very existence of the community as a whole.

The Florentine constitution, as it had existed for two centuries, was a thing of pretence and make-believe, as one historian has expressed it, aimed to create the illusion of a republic on what was in fact a monarchy. Florence recognised that a one-man government was essential but at the same time denied that one man the necessary apparatus of government. 'It was not the fault of Lorenzo if he was ever seeking to harmonize the facts of life by the constitutional fictions by which he was continually hampered. It was the fault of Florence that she desired to enjoy concurrently the advantages of monarchy and republicanism, having proved herself unfitted for true republicanism, while making monarchy impossible by insisting upon the retention of the forms of a republican constitution. No man could have satisfied the prime requirements of Florence except one who could at one and the same time be a monarch and a private person, a citizen and a prince, a burgher-merchant and the chief representative of the State. He must fashion all the political bricks and compact them into a sure edifice of rule, but any demand for constitutional straw might be construed as high treason, as evidence of a fell design to uproot the liberties of his country.'

Lorenzo's first constitutional move was to create a new body. A *Balia* was

197

initiated by the *Signoria* which, composed of two hundred and seventy-seven carefully-selected persons, represented a large section of Florentine opinion. It was given the authority to carry out necessary reforms and, in a week, had authorised the setting-up of a new Council of Seventy, composed of the thirty original members of the *Balia* and of forty others chosen by them. Future vacancies were to be filled by co-option. This Council was given virtual control of all branches of government. It was to select the *Signoria* and Colleges, to decide what laws should be introduced and to appoint from its own members two new Committees, one consisting of eight members, the *Otto di Practica*, in charge of foreign affairs, and the other of twelve, the *Dodici Procuratori*, concerned with commerce and finance. It was also responsible for the organ of penal jurisdiction, the *Otto di Balia*. The result of these changes was to give the supreme authority in the Republic to an inner ring of *cittadini del stato* as they were called, virtually all of them Medici supporters. Also, and more importantly, continuity was assured, for though the new powers were bestowed for five years only, they were renewed in 1484 and again in 1489, so that they were continuously in force till after Lorenzo's death.

The extent to which the Council of Seventy overshadowed in prestige even the *Signoria* was shown by the enactment that if a Gonfalonier of Justice was exceptionally good in his term of office (normally, it will be remembered, two months) he might be rewarded by a place among the Seventy. The Gonfalonier of the Republic of the moment was an *ex officio* member of the council. The attempt to make the Seventy genuinely representative of Florence can be seen from the stipulations that, of the Forty, each member should have reached the age of forty; that no two members of the same family could sit among the Forty; that if a family was already represented in the Thirty it could have no representative in the Forty; that the full Council of Seventy should represent the Greater Guilds and the Lesser Guilds in the proportion of three-fourths and one-fourth; that the members of the Greater Guilds must have qualified for the office of Gonfalonier of Justice; and that no member could vote unless his taxes were paid in full.

For convenience's sake – for seventy was too large a number for certain delicate manipulations – the Council was divided into two sections, each of thirty-five members. Each section acted alone and in turn for a year, care being taken that each section should consist of the full complement of thirty-five persons.

On the inner ring, the two Committees, the Eight for foreign affairs and the Twelve for home, members were not eligible for re-election when their six-months' term was up and in consequence every member of the Seventy gained, in the course of a few years, personal and practical experience in the

Pope Sixtus IV giving blessings : school of Melozzo.

conduct of affairs. Every measure of the *Signoria* had to be submitted to the appropriate Committee, which either sanctioned it or returned it for debate to the Seventy as a whole, whose decision was final. Every act of government, diplomatic, legislative or economic, had to be approved by a two-thirds majority of the Seventy, sitting in conclave, two-thirds of the members being present. When so approved – and only then – the measure was allowed to proceed on its old, accustomed course through the *Signoria*, the successive Councils of the People, the Commune and the Hundred.

The result of the new constitution was a government far more representative of Florence than any modern 'Parliamentary democracy'. The provisions about families and the two-thirds quorums were sufficient guarantees against despotism and dictatorship. Whatever exactly the Seventy were, they were not picked partisans of Lorenzo, for among them was his personal enemy, the sour republican Alemanno Rinuccini, who, of course, complained that the change marked the death of popular liberty. Lorenzo's enemies spread the rumour that he intended to alter the required age for a Gonfalonier (which was forty-five) and get himself made Gonfalonier for life; but, as he made no plans for his own future except, according to Poliziano who was in a position to know, to retire from public life in favour of his eldest son, Pietro, the rumour may be dismissed for the 'popular' propaganda that it was.

The Pope and his son Girolamo Riario, still intent on the murder of Lorenzo, managed to find in Florence a sufficient number of venal 'patriots', acting under the Frescobaldi who had been the Florentine representative at Constantinople and who considered that Lorenzo was not sufficiently grateful to him for having procured the return of Giuliano's murderer, to undertake to murder him. The pattern of the earlier attempt was to be followed and Lorenzo was to be assassinated when he attended Mass on Ascension Day, June 3, 1481. But this time, the conspiracy was discovered in time and all those involved in it in Florence were executed on June 6. Henceforth any attempt on his life was pronounced High Treason and his unique position implicitly recognised.

The *Signoria* assigned to him a special bodyguard and henceforth Lorenzo de' Medici was recognised by all Italy and the world as the accredited and almost princely representative of the Florentine State. He became 'the needle of the Italian compass' and, despite the Pope's efforts to keep the war going to further aggrandise Girolamo Riario, Lorenzo managed to frame a peace between Naples, Milan and Venice. When Sixtus heard of it, he 'became speechless with fury' and on the following day – August 12, 1484 – to the relief of all Italy he died.

Lorenzo thereupon sent an embassy to the new Pope, Giambattista Cibò, who took the name of Innocent VIII, which included his eldest son, Pietro, who was now fourteen, in the charge of Poliziano. Pietro's business was to turn the new Pope's mind to the item of policy which had never been absent from Lorenzo's mind since he himself had originally broached it to Sixtus – the bestowal of a Cardinal's Hat on the second son of the family. His own second son was now seven years old.

Giovanni was already in minor orders (a technicality which enabled him legally to hold a benefice) and he was Archbishop of Aix in Provence (which gave him a substantial income). Lorenzo reported it: 'On May 19, we received the intelligence that the King of France had presented to my son Giovanni, the Abbey of Fontedolce. On the 31st we heard from Rome that the Pope had confirmed the grant and had rendered him capable of holding a benefice, he being now seven years old. On June 1, I took Giovanni from Poggio a Caiano to Florence where he was confirmed by the Bishop of Arezzo in the chapel of our family, and received the tonsure; and from thenceforth was called 'Messire Giovanni'. The next day we returned to Poggio. On June 8 arrived letters from the King of France saying that he had conferred upon

Left: *Lorenzo's eldest son Pietro: portrait by Perugino.* Right: *Angelo Poliziano: part of a fresco by Ghirlandaio.*

Messire Giovanni the Archbishopric of Aix in Provence.'

Lorenzo gave careful instructions to his eldest son Pietro how to proceed on his brother's behalf: 'After having given my commendations to His Holiness, you will inform him that your affection for your brother induces you to speak a word in his favour. You can here mention that I have educated him for the priesthood, and shall closely attend to his learning and manners, so that he may not disgrace his profession; that, in this respect, I rest all my hopes on His Holiness who, having already given us proofs of his kindness and affection, will add to our obligations by any promotion which he may think proper to bestow upon him; endeavouring by these and similar expressions to commend your brother to his favour as much as lies in your power.'

It was a long letter, modelled obviously on the instructions which Lorenzo's father had been in the habit of writing to him, and there is no passage more characteristic than his opening: 'On your arrival in Rome be most careful not to take precedence of your countrymen who are your superiors in age, for though you are my son you will remember that you are only a citizen of Florence like themselves.'

En Famille

Lorenzo's determination to get a Cardinalate for his second son represented the climax of his ambition for his family – not particularly on account of the status in itself but because it was essential for the arbiter of Italian policy to have some firm link with Rome. It was probable that, once the College of Cardinals was infiltrated, the Papacy itself was within the Medici grasp. And Giovanni, of course, was eventually to become that Pope Leo X whose first words on hearing that he was elected are reported to have been: 'As God has seen fit to give us the Papacy, let us enjoy it.'

No word is preserved of gratitude for his father's mundane efforts, which were considerable and involved an arduous diplomatic campaign and the outlay of much money. At one stage the possibility was discussed of erasing from the register the date of Giovanni's baptism and of producing witnesses to swear that he was two years older than he in fact was. The bestowal on him of the Abbey of Monte Cassino by King Ferrante and that of Miromondo by Ludovico *Il Moro* when he was eleven were tokens of amity from Naples and Milan to Florence and at least made some impression on the College of Cardinals, so that when Pope Innocent finally consented to bestow the Cardinalate on the boy at the unprecedented age of thirteen, it was only the Venetian Cardinal Barbo who objected. It was in the March of 1489 that Giovanni's name was included in the list of promotions, with the proviso that, under pain of excommunication, the nomination was not to be made public until after a lapse of three years. Nevertheless, Lorenzo heard of it on the day that the appointment was made and wrote immediately to his ambassador in Rome: 'This is the greatest achievement of our House.' So also thought the foreign ambassadors who were in Florence and crowded to the Medici palace to pay their compliments. The Cardinalate was proof enough of Lorenzo's influence at the Vatican and the man who had the Pope in his pocket was the man to conciliate and, if possible, to use.

For the three years of waiting, Giovanni was sent to the University of

Pisa, where he graduated in Canon Law. As the clever child of the family (Lorenzo said to his three sons that Pietro was foolish, Giovanni clever and the youngest, Giuliano, good) he had been carefully educated from the first, though the quarrel between Poliziano and Clarice as to whether Giovanni should learn Latin from sacred or from secular texts resulted in the appointment of another tutor for him and the man who was chosen, Bernardo Michelozzi, the son of the architect, was a man of wide rather than deep learning and pandered to Giovanni's natural dilettantism. Giovanni's interests were extremely varied – theology, law, the classical poets and orators, poetry in the vernacular and mathematics, as well as a love of music and painting.

As a step towards the Hat, Giovanni's sister, Maddalena, was pressed into service by their father. The new Pope was an affable easy-going Genoese with several children – he was the first Pope openly to acknowledge his offspring and not pretend that his sons were his 'nephews' – and Lorenzo decided that a marriage between the families might make things easier. Accordingly it was arranged that Innocent VIII's eldest son, Franceschetto Cibò, should marry Maddalena, Lorenzo's second daughter, who was her mother's favourite child and, indeed, much resembled Clarice in her invalidism and lack of any intellectual interests. She was fourteen and her bridegroom was about forty, a gambler and a profligate, who had managed to get himself made a Captain-General, which had prompted his future father-in-law to write to a friend: 'I think he should not pursue mere smoke. A captain ought to have seen some service and made himself a reputation. I wish he had sought to secure a maintenance and I wonder it does not strike him that the day after the Pope dies he will be the poorest man on earth, and I shall have to provide for him and his wife.'

Nevertheless in the November of 1487, Maddalena, accompanied by her mother and her brother Pietro set out for Rome where the Pope himself performed the ceremony.

With them went Jacopo Salviati, a nephew of that Archbishop of Pisa who was prominent in the Pazzi conspiracy. He was shortly to become the husband of Lucrezia, Lorenzo's eldest daughter and, of all his children the most like him in character, thus healing the mortal breach between the families. Lucrezia was as forceful as Maddalena was colourless. From her earliest years she had given proof of her energy and intellect. She wrote lively letters to her grandmother, the elder Lucrezia, many of whose religious poems she knew by heart. Among her childish requests are 'the basket of roses you promised me' and sugar plums for her younger brothers and sisters. Another, more recondite, was for a sash made from the pallium of St John. Her habit of asking favours for her friends and something of her father's directness

remained throughout her life, as did her temperamental dislike of Maddalena which, after Lorenzo's death, split the family into rival camps.

Lorenzo's third daughter, Luigia, was betrothed to her Medici cousin of the younger branch of the family in the hope of healing that growing rift but she died suddenly before her wedding. The fourth girl, Contessina, named after her great-grandmother, Cosmo's wife, was still a child when Lorenzo died. Their eldest brother, Pietro, gives a picture of his sisters in a letter to their father written when he was about eight: 'Lucrezia sews, sings and reads; Maddalena goes knocking her head against the walls but somehow manages not to hurt herself; Luigia can already say several little sentences; Contessina is making a great noise all over the house.'

The sudden death of Luigia in the spring of 1488 caused the postponement of the next family marriage which was that of Pietro to Alfonsina Orsini, whose father had died in the service of King Ferrante who had allowed the wedding to take place by proxy in the royal palace of Naples in February and had himself attended it in state. Lorenzo, in making this particular alliance, was in all probability thinking of Naples rather than Rome which had been in his mind – or, rather, in his father's – when the first Orsini alliance was contracted, his own marriage to Clarice. The Orsini in themselves proved a liability rather than a strength to the Medici.

That July, shortly after the festivities which eventually marked the marriage of Pietro and Alfonsina and which were attended by Franceschetto and Maddalena, Clarice died. The Ferrarese ambassador correctly evaluated it when he informed his master of the event three days later and explained the delay by saying that he did not send the news immediately as it did not seem to him to be of much importance. She was not quite forty.

Lorenzo was not with his wife when she died, but himself taking the baths at Macereto in Sienese territory. One of his friends wrote immediately to the Florentine ambassador at Rome: 'If you should hear Lorenzo blamed for not being at his wife's death, make excuses for him. Leoni his physician considered it imperative for his health to go to the baths and no one had any idea that Madonna Clarice's death was so near.' She was entombed in San Lorenzo the evening after she died and the solemn obsequies, at which the whole city was present, took place on August 1. Henceforth Lorenzo, having to play a dual part, seems to have become even more bound to his children.

The year after Clarice's death when Lorenzo was taking the baths once more at Spedelatto, he wrote to his 'dear little Contessina' who, aged eleven, was in Florence with no one but Alfonsina and her baby for company, and was asking when he was coming home. He assured her that it would not be

Opposite: *Statue of Pope Innocent VIII by Pollaiolo.*

long before he would be with her, restored to health again and as well as ever he had been. Meanwhile she must pray God for him and herself keep well and happy. The boys should not have gone and left her, but meanwhile she must keep Alfonsina company and tell her from him to take great care of the baby.

Lorenzo's desire to keep Maddalena with him when at last her husband brought her to Florence just before Clarice's death was so great that he instructed his representative to gain the Pope's help: 'I should be glad if you could mention the matter to His Holiness and get it arranged that Maddalena should remain here for the rest of the summer and autumn. I have not so far had time to see my daughter comfortably, so I earnestly beg His Holiness that of his kindness he will let me have her a few months more.'

Innocent accommodatingly sent his son on a mission to Perugia so that Maddalena might remain in Florence and Lorenzo thanked him: 'You can imagine what comfort Clarice finds in the presence of the daughter who has always been the apple of her eye. We are both very grateful to Your Holiness. Of myself I say nothing, for you know how I love all my children.'

Franceschetto Cibò, when he made his first visit to Florence, accompanying his new brother-in-law, Pietro de' Medici and his bride back from Rome, received his first lesson in the domestic regimen of Lorenzo. The Pope's son had brought with him an elaborate retinue, composed of many members of the highest Roman families, and they were all luxuriously entertained at one of the Florentine palaces. After three days, however, Cibò and Maddalena went to the Medici palace to stay with Lorenzo and Clarice. There, astonished at the simple style of living, so different from what he had been accustomed to in the Vatican as well as from that which his suite was still receiving, Franceschetto thought that he was being deliberately insulted and Lorenzo had to explain to him that what was intended was the very reverse of a slight. Luxurious entertainment was lavished only on guests, whereas he and Maddalena were no guests but members of the family.

The family link, however, had no noticeable effect on the Pope who insisted on Giovanni's Cardinalate being kept a secret until he had completed the specified three years at the university. Lorenzo could see no reason why the boy's assumption of his office should be deferred and his impatience was increased considerably by the news, in the autumn of 1490, that Innocent had had an apoplectic fit. The Pope, however, recovered and, with his convalescence, came also an annoyance at Lorenzo's constant appeals to him to change his mind. He could not know that Lorenzo, already far gone with the

Opposite: *Portrait of Lorenzo the Magnificent by Bronzino.*

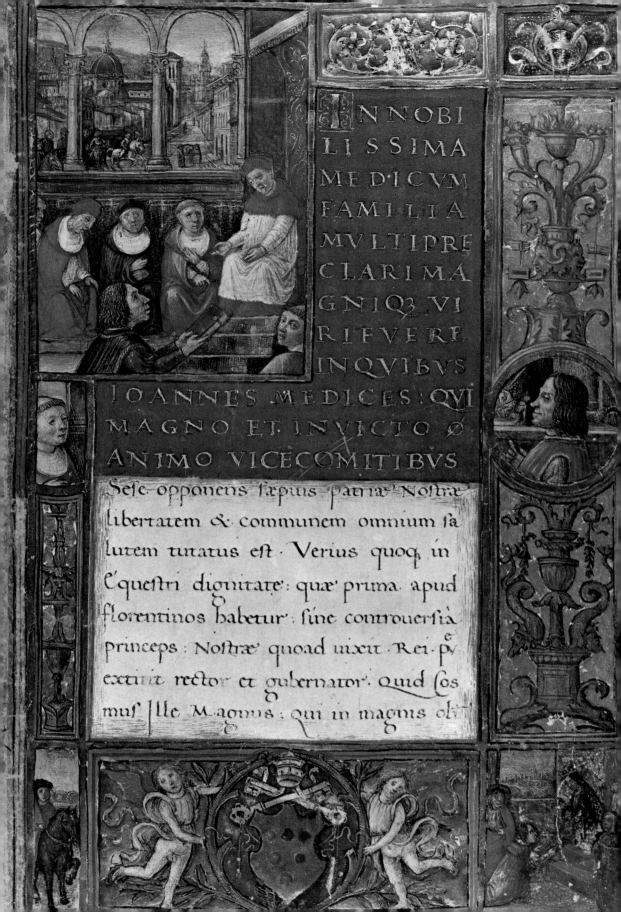

INNOBI
LISSIMA
MEDICVM
FAMILIA
MVLTIPRE
CLARIMA
GNIQ3 VI
RI FVERE
IN QVIBVS
IOANNES MEDICES: QVI
MAGNO ET INVICTO Ō
ANIMO VICECOMITIBVS

Sese opponens saepius patriae Nostrae
libertatem & communem omnium sa
lutem tutatus est. Verius quoq; in
Equestri dignitate: quae prima apud
florentinos habetur: sine controuersia
princeps: Nostrae quoad uixit Rei p̄
extitit rector et gubernator. Quid Cos
mus Ille Magnus: qui in magnis ob̄

family's hereditary gout, feared that he himself might not live to see his son's triumph.

There was also his fear for his children's health which, though he hid it stoically enough from the world in general, was not unknown to the man who best knew his heart. Poliziano, indeed, on one occasion when Pietro was ill, had communicated the news not direct to him but to Michelozzi and drawn from Lorenzo the sad rebuke: 'Can you really imagine that my temper is so infirm as to be disturbed by the news? If my nature were so weak as to be disturbed by every wind, yet experience has taught me to brave the storm. I have not only known what it is to bear the sickness and even the death of some of my children, but the untimely death of my father when I was only twenty so much exposed me to the attacks of fortune that life became a burden to me. Surely you should know that if Nature denied me strength, Experience has by now remedied the defect.'

It was not, in fact, until thirty days before Lorenzo's own death that, in the March of 1492, Giovanni was inducted into the Cardinalate in the Abbey of Fiesole. Lorenzo was too ill to attend the ceremony, but waited to receive his son in the Medici palace when the great procession, escorted by Pietro, arrived in Florence. According to an eye-witness, 'the whole city, nay, the whole territory, was gathered together, as one man, from which it may be judged how earnestly this dignity had been desired for one of the citizens of Florence.' On the following day in the Duomo, the 'Red Mass' – the Mass of the Holy Spirit – was sung by eight bishops in the presence of the new Cardinal; and afterwards a great banquet was given in the Medici palace. Lorenzo was too ill to attend either gathering, but he had himself carried into the great hall to see the company of sixty notables which had come to honour 'our Monsignore'. To his eyes, Giovanni seemed 'to have changed since yesterday'. There was only one more thing the father could do. He would write his son a letter of advice, distilling paternal wisdom.

As extracts of this letter have been quoted, usually out of context, by all Lorenzo's biographers (including one who sees it as an amusing first draft of Polonius's speech to Laertes), it is necessary to give it in full, for any comprehension of Lorenzo's character.

'Messire Giovanni', it runs, 'you and we on your behalf owe great thankfulness to our Lord God. For over and above many honours and benefits bestowed on our house, He has granted to it in your person the highest dignity to which it has ever risen. The matter, great enough in itself, is made far greater by the circumstances of your youth and our position. The first

Opposite: *A page of dedication to Giovanni de' Medici's cardinalate, from Niccolo Valori's* Vita di Lorenzo il Magnifico.

thing, therefore, that I want to impress on you is that you never forget to be grateful to God, remembering always that it is not through *your* merits or *your* wisdom that you gained this dignity, but through His favour. This you must recognise and give proof of your recognition by leading a virtuous, exemplary and chaste life. To this you are all the more bound because in your youth you have already given signs of such conduct and it would be a shame for you and a sad disappointment for me if you should forget your good beginning at an age when others are arriving at discretion and regularity in their conduct. You must therefore try to lighten the burden of the dignity bestowed on you by real perseverance in the studies befitting your profession.

'During the past year, it has given me much comfort to hear that, without being urged by anyone and entirely of your own accord, you had regularly gone to confession and received the Blessed Sacrament at Mass. I believe there is no better way of continuing in the grace of God than by persevering in these practices. This is the first and the most important advice I have to give. But as you are going to live in Rome, that sink of all iniquity, I realise that you will find it very hard to follow it. For not only does example have an influence on everyone, but you personally will have no lack of evil counsellors and tempters.

'As you can quite understand, your elevation to the Cardinalate so young excites great envy. Those who have not been successful in preventing you receiving that honour will do their best subtly to diminish its value by trying to make your manner of life appear in an unfavourable light and to drag you down into the pit into which they themselves are fallen. They assume that your youth will make this easier for them. You must be very much on your guard against them, remembering in these days there is little virtue in the members of the Sacred College, though I can remember that once the College was filled with holy and learned men, whose example you should try to emulate.

'At the same time as you endeavour to follow the virtuous examples of the men of old, you must beware lest in avoiding the Scylla of evil behaviour you fall into the Charybdis of hypocrisy. Cultivate moderation and in both your conduct and your speech, avoid offending others by too great a laxity and by too great an austerity. You will understand this in time better than I can explain it to you.

'You will have no difficulty in seeing how much depends on the personality and example of a cardinal. If all cardinals were what they should be, the world would be a better place, for it would mean there was always a good Pope who would ensure the peace of Christendom. Strive yourself, therefore, to be such that if all the rest were to imitate you we should be able to anticipate this universal boon.

210

'Today I have given you up wholly to God and His Holy Church. Therefore you must become a good priest and convince everyone that you prefer the welfare and honour of the Church and the Apostolic See to all the things of this world and all private considerations and interests. If you keep this steadily before your eyes, you will find you do not lack opportunity of serving both the city and your house. For the alliance with the Church is advantageous to the city. You must form the link between the two; and though the future cannot be foreseen I believe we shall not lack means on both sides if you hold fast to this most important resolution that I am urging on you – to place the Church before everything else.

'You are the youngest member of the Sacred College, not only at the present moment but of all that have hitherto been created. Therefore it is essential that when you meet the other cardinals you should be the most humble and unassuming, never causing others to wait for you in the Chapel or the Consistory or on deputations. You will soon get to know which of your colleagues are the least and which the most dependable. You will have to avoid confidential discussions with those of evil lives, not only because of the thing itself, but because of public opinion. But on general topics you should talk freely to them all.

'When you have to appear in public, either on solemn occasions or when you are entertaining, I suggest that it is advisable for you to moderate your enthusiasm rather than to overstep it. I should prefer a well-filled stable and well-ordered, cleanly servants to a display of pomp and riches. Try to live with regularity, reducing your expenses gradually with those limits which may not at first be possible. Silk and jewels are suitable for your position in certain circumstances only; far more suitable are a few good antiquities and some fine books. The society you surround yourself with should be learned and respectable rather than numerous; at the same time you should invite others to your house more often than you accept invitations to theirs. Eat plain food and take plenty of exercise; for (for want of them) those of your cloth quickly contract many illnesses for which there is no cure.

'The position of a cardinal is not only lofty but secure, so that it often happens that those who obtain it become careless, saying to themselves that they have gained their objective and assuming that they will be able to retain it without any trouble, and this often does serious harm to the life and character. I advise you to be as careful as possible and to have rather too little than too much confidence in your own strength.

'One rule of life I urge on you before all others: Get up early every morn-

Overleaf: *The interior of the Abbey of Fiesole, where Giovanni de' Medici was finally inducted into the Cardinalate a month after his father's death.*

211

his own experience for the characters of both the young Julian and the old Constantine and the play is as much his political testament to them (as well as *apologia* for himself) as his private letters.

Since the statue of Victory was taken away from the Curia – so speaks Julian – success no longer crowns the Roman arms which once subdued the world. Only by recalling the old gods can we recall Victory to our standards. But this object will not be attained by this alone, or by taking from the Christians the wealth and possessions which were forbidden them by their own faith. The head of the Empire must once more command the old reverence and this is impossible if the ruler hands over to others the cares of government, while he heaps up treasure and thinks only of amusement. If he is rich, his riches are but lent to him to share with his people and relieve necessity wherever he finds it.

> *La Signoria, la roba Impero*
> *Già non è sua, anzi del popolo tutto*
> *E benchè del Signor paia lo'ntero*
> *Non è, nè'l posseder, nè l'usufrutto*
> *Ma distributore è'l Signor vero.*

which has been Englished in such a way as to stress its affinity with later political ideas:

> The government and the imperial sway
> Are not his own by any right divine:
> They are but symbols of the people's will.
> To outward view he is the Lord of all,
> Yet he is Lord in truth who is content
> To administer a delegated power,
> Nor claim possession, usufruct or right.

The ruler must know how to hold an even balance; he must eschew both meanness and luxury; he must be *affabil, dolce e grato* and the servant of those he serves. How little do his subjects know

> *Quanto affanno e doglia*
> *Dà il regno di che avete tanta voglia*

'what cares and griefs come from that crown which men so much desire'.

There can be so little doubt that, as far as the art of governing is concerned, Lorenzo is speaking in his own person through the mouths of Constantine and Julian, that it is impossible not to speculate whether other judgments are not equally personal. His attitude, for example, to astrology?

Il re e'l savio so sopra le stelle
Ond'io son fuor di questa vana legge
I buoni punti e le buone ore son quelle
Che l'uomo felice da se elegee.

He makes, in flat defiance of history, Julian say in repudiation of his known habit of consulting the stars – 'the king and the sage are above the stars, so I dissociate myself from this vain custom. Good moves and good moments are those which the fortunate man chooses for himself.' Was Lorenzo here repudiating his friend Pico della Mirandola who in that year 1487 – he was twenty-four – had gone to Rome to post nine hundred theses for public debate on his great synthesis of Scripture, neo-Platonism, the Orphic hymns, the Chaldean oracles and the Cabala, astrology and other occult methods of foretelling the future, dreams, sibyls and portents as well as the flight and intestines of birds? Pico's purpose was to show how everything concurred in proving the divinity of Christ. The Pope could not be expected to see it like that. Innocent VIII had a mania about the occult and in 1484 had commissioned two devout Dominicans to write a long and detailed attack, *Malleus Maleficarum*, 'The Witches' Hammer', which spread widely and became the classic formulation for centuries of the Church's case against sorcery.

At such a moment it might well be that Lorenzo would not wish to be seen in opposition to Innocent and at the same time would not disown his friends and much of the teaching, properly understood, with which he agreed. Was the speech in the play an escape from the dilemma?

Even more intriguing is the passage in which Constantine, lamenting the deaths of his brothers, is comforted by the reflection that perhaps it is all for the best as his brothers, had they lived, might have proved a source of danger to him:

> . . . *nascer suole*
> *Discordia tra fratei molte fiate,*
> *Forse che la Fortuna te gli ha tolti*
> *Acciocchè in te sol sio quel ch'era in molti.*

'For between brothers discords oft arise.
Perchance the Fate was kind that robbed thee of them
Seeing that on thee alone the duty falls
Which others inconveniently would have shared.'

Had Lorenzo, with the passage of time, so consoled himself for the intolerable hurt of the murder of the beloved Giuliano? After Giuliano he named his youngest son who was only ten when Lorenzo died but was even then the favourite of his brothers and sisters. In later years he became Duke of Nemours and was showered with honours by Giovanni as Pope Leo. Giuliano was, by Giovanni's orders, buried in the New Sacristy of San Lorenzo. His monument, representing him as Gonfalonier of the Papal Forces, was sculpted by Michelangelo.

The boy, Michelangelo, a year or two older than Giuliano, was in Lorenzo's last years attached to the family. Lorenzo discovered him in the Medici garden at San Marco with its collection of antique statuary (which was open to all artists as the Laurentian Library was free to all scholars) copying the head of a faun, having borrowed a chisel and begged a piece of marble from some masons at work there. Impressed by the boy's promise, Lorenzo sent for his father and arranged that he should live *en famille* at the Medici palace to devote himself to sculpture, 'showing the results of his labours to *Il Magnifico* each day'. It was Lorenzo's custom to take his dinner with his sons, other members of the household and any guests who cared to drop in, and the rule was that the first arrivals, whatever their age or status, sat next to the master of the house. The youthful genius was punctual to enjoy the privilege and the frequent spectacle of Lorenzo with Poliziano on one side and Michelangelo on the other was a reminder of the meaning of the patronage of the Medici.

Much of the summer was spent at the new villa Lorenzo built at Poggio a Caiano and celebrated his mythological poem, *Ambra*, written in imitation of Ovid's *Metamorphoses*. The villa was on a rocky eminence, rising from the Ombrone river not far from its junction with the Arno, and Lorenzo tells of a nymph, Ambra, beloved of the shepherd Lauro and protected by the goddess Diana. As Ambra was bathing in the clear waters of the streams, the river god Ombrone espied and pursued her. 'Her fears adding wings to her white feet', she fled until she reached the spot where Ombrone and Arno meet. There Ombrone called on his brother Arno to prevent her further flight, but the nymph in despair invoked Diana and was turned into a rock.

Her prayer runs:

> *Diana bello, questo petto casto*
> *Non maculò giammai folle disio,*
> *Guardalo or tu, perch'io Ninfa non basto*
> *A duo nemici, e l'uno e l'altro Dio.*
> *Col desio del morir m'è sol rimasto*
> *Al core il casto amor di Lauro mio*
> *Portate, o venti, questa voce estrema*
> *A Lauro mio, che la mia morte gema.*

Translated to keep the rhyming scheme of *ottava rima,*

Beauteous Diana, shall it not avail
   That never spot hath stained this breast of mine?
Protect me. I a Nymph cannot prevail
   Against two foes and each of them Divine.
Now as I die no fears of death assail
   Save for the love I bear Lorenzo mine.
      Carry, oh winds, to him my latest breath
      That he a little while shall mourn my death!

The Medici family's villa of Poggio a Caiano.

Marsilio Ficino, from a fresco by Ghirlandaio.

Ambra contains some of Lorenzo's best descriptions of nature, the vein in which he was the unquestioned master, depicting the countryside after the harvest is gathered and the migrant birds have gone overseas, the rivers are swollen and the trees bare. As the floods rise, the frightened peasant frees his cattle from their stalls and seeks safety, carrying his goods on his back and his weeping child in his arms.

> *Alcun della famiglia s'è ridotto*
> *In cima delle case; e su del tetto*
> *La povera ricchezza vede ir sotto,*
> *La fatica, la speme; e per sospetto*
> *Di se stesso non duolsi e non fa motto;*
> *Teme alla vita il cor nel tristo petto,*
> *Nè delle cose car par conto faccia;*
> *Così la maggior cura ogni altra caccia.*

'Some take refuge at the top of their houses, and from the roof see their poor wealth being carried away, and with it their toil and their hope; anxious for their own safety, they neither lament nor speak. The heart in each sad breast fears for life and seems to take no heed of cherished possessions, the greater trouble drives out all others.'

In the same *ottava rima*, Lorenzo wrote a light and amusing poem of the countryside on the subject of a hawking party at his villa, *La Caccia col Falcone*. It tells of a day devoted to falconry. As *Ambra* opens with a picture of winter, so *La Caccia* describes the dawn, the east all touched with red, while the mountain tops gleamed all of gold. The hawkers are astir early preparing for the arrival of their masters. The dogs, each called by its own name, gather to the cry and soon a brilliant company assembles. The dogs draw the coverts – *Tira, buon can, su, tira su, cammina* – and the hawks and falcons flash upon their prey. Two hawkers have a violent quarrel over the behaviour of their respective birds but are eventually reconciled – an incident which is said to have been the actual event on which the poem is founded. *La Caccia* ends with the return of the exhausted company in the heat of the day.

Though Lorenzo is said to have preferred hawks to falcons, Poliziano, in one of his letters, records: 'Yesterday we went hawking. It was windy and we were unlucky, for we lost Pilato's falcon called Montovano. Today we tried again and again the wind was contrary; yet we had some fine flights, for Maestro Giorgio let loose his falcon, which returned obediently at the given signal. Lorenzo is quite in love with the bird, and not without reason, for Maestro Giorgio says he has never seen one larger or finer, and he hopes to make him the finest falcon in the world. While we were in the field Pilato returned from the shore with the truant of yesterday, which redoubled Lorenzo's pleasure. We are hawking from morning to night and do nothing else, though on Monday I hear our sport is to be varied by a deer-hunt.'

For riding-horses, hunters and racers, Lorenzo had, as has been mentioned, a life-long passion. In the October of 1488, he bought twenty mares at Naples and only a short time before his death horses from Egypt and from the Barbary Coast were on their way to him. His favourite racer, which was always victorious, he named from its dark colour, Morello. It was so attached to him that it showed signs of illness when he did not feed it with his own hand and always showed its joy at his approach by loud neighing and stamping.

But the countrified Lorenzo was much more than a nature-poet (though here in world-literature he can claim equality with Wordsworth and Tennyson) or the lover of sport. He was the landed proprietor, taking an intelligent interest in every branch of requisite skill. He mastered the difficulties of drainage, breeds of stock, tree-planting. He procured from Sicily a special breed of golden pheasant and from Calabria a particularly fine breed of pigs. His cows were famous throughout Italy and he was able to supply Florence with a new and superior brand of cheese to supplant that imported from Lombardy. He bred large quantities of silkworms for commercial purposes.

More and more, he transferred his interests from commerce and banking (for which it appears he had neither the interest nor the aptitude of his father and grandfather), to the real wealth of agriculture; and when the Republic, in gratitude for the enormous amounts of his own money he had expended on the State which he had saved, remitted his own incidental debts, Lorenzo decided that he would no longer remain at the mercy of dishonest, idle and venal agents and factors of his European business interests, but would look for another way of ruling. But, in retiring to the country and leaving Piero to undertake the burdens of the Medici business, he remained the guardian of Florence, deserving of the tribute of Poliziano's poem, *Sylva*, written (in Latin) to him:

> Then free from babbling crowds and city noise
> You sing the pleasures rural life enjoys
> Or with no faltering step pursue your way
> To touch the confines of celestial day
> – These the delights your happiest moments share
> Your certain palliatives of public care;
> Blest in your genius; your capacious mind
> Not to one science or one theme confined
> By grateful interchange fatigue beguiles
> In private studies and in public toils.

Lorenzo and Italy

It has been perspicaciously said of Lorenzo that during the last twelve years of his life, from 1480 to 1492, there were few if any 'great events' to record, though the time is full of events of great importance. To the casual observer Florence seemed to be enjoying the happiness which is said to come of having no history and the real interest of Lorenzo's life is within in his own spiritual and artistic development, not in incidents with which he was externally associated.

Guicciardini opens his great contemporary history with the remark that the time of Lorenzo was 'prosperous beyond any other which Italy had experienced during the long course of a hundred years' and, after a long panegyric, he says that this 'was by general consent ascribed to the industry and virtue of Lorenzo de' Medici'. More particularly, realising that Lorenzo's achievement lay in his ability to keep the rival states at peace, he compared him to the isthmus of Corinth, a piece of solid land which alone prevented turbulent seas from dashing against each other.

In the vaster perspective of history, the rule of Lorenzo is a golden age which has the nature of a sunset. With his death the warring states ensured that Italy declined from being the centre of European civilisation to being the cockpit of the Continent which the 'new' powers – Spain, Germany, France and England – devastated in search of plunder.

Italy had been the Continent in little. Not only did its states exhibit every form of government – the Neapolitan monarchy in the south, the Papal theocracy in the centre and in the north the Venetian oligarchy, the Florentine republic and the Milanese despotism, as well as the varying constitutions of the smaller states – but the Big Five, by their shifting alliances and their *condottieri* wars, were intent on maintaining a balance of power in the peninsula without anything but a passing reference to the 'barbarian' (or, to use the modern term, 'developing') world beyond the Alps.

Unfortunately that world, by force of circumstances, was too much with

225

them. Through trade and discovery, through the drive for expansion and the intermarriage of dynasties, they were irrevocably involved in Europe and though the actual invitation to the French to invade Italy was the work of Ludovico *Il Moro* of Milan two years after Lorenzo's death, other states were, in their own ways, participators in the crime which devastated the peninsula, led to a new sack of Rome and caused a native poet to voice the general lamentation with: 'What madness led you, my beloved Italy, to pour out Latin blood for the sake of barbarians?'

Ferrante of Naples by his ferocious rule had driven into exile at the court of France many powerful nobles who never ceased to urge Louis XI's successor, Charles VIII, a repulsive youth of twenty-two, to assert his tenuous claim to Naples and Sicily and to invade Italy, which he eventually did, considering himself a new Charlemagne and was welcomed as the Lord's Anointed by the half-mad epileptic Dominican Savonarola, who gained power in Florence after Lorenzo's death.

But as long as Lorenzo lived, there was no foreign invasion. Nor, because of his realisation that the Pope was the master-key to Italian unity, were there the dangerous inter-state wars of earlier years. The war between Venice and the Papal allies over Ferrara was ended by the peace of Bagnolo in the August of 1484 and the death of Pope Sixtus IV the same month (from an apoplectic rage that his own and his son, Girolamo Riario's, efforts to stir up war had failed) meant that, with the accession of Innocent VIII, Lorenzo's influence for general peace increased. It was he who had summoned and attended the Conference of Cremona despite Louis XI's warning that Girolamo Riario would make another murder attempt. The so-called 'Barons' War', between Ferrante and the Papacy, ended in 1486 after the Neapolitan victory at Montorio, mainly because of Lorenzo's diplomatic efforts which had also prevented the struggle becoming a general conflagration, joined by Venice and Milan. And three years later Florence regained its northern fortress of Sarzana (which had been lost in the Pazzi war) with the minimum of military pressure.

The innumerable letters written to Innocent both by Lorenzo himself and by his secretary, Piero da Bibbiena, bear witness to Lorenzo's unrelenting efforts to keep control of the Pope – and thus (quite apart from Giovanni's Hat) to control the policies of Italy. He succeeded to an extent which caused the Ferrarese envoy at the Vatican to remark, 'His Holiness sleeps with the eyes of *Il Magnifico* Lorenzo.' And the *savoir faire* of Lorenzo's despatches was of less importance than the *savoir vivre* which led him to discover that Innocent had a passion for ortolans and, in consequence, to order that every courier from Florence to Rome should bring ortolans for the Pope. To this he occasionally added flagons of the famous wine, Vernaccia; though this was more probably an indulgence of his own sense of humour. Lorenzo, as one of the foremost Dante scholars of Italy, would certainly have known – as Innocent would not have known – that the poet had condemned an earlier Pope to Purgatory because of his overfondness for it. When Lorenzo said that he had no greater wish than to keep the Pope merry and content, he gave the recipe for the pacification of Italy in the prevailing circumstances.

More concretely, in the year 1488 when the wretched Girolamo Riario was murdered in Forli and the banner of the Church was raised to avenge him, Innocent failed to give the expected help. A month after the murder in Forli came that of Manfredi, Lord of Faenza, who was stabbed to death in his wife's bedroom by assassins she had engaged for the purpose, as the prelude to an attempt by her father, the *condottiere* of Milan, to bring Faenza under Milanese domination. Lorenzo intervened to guarantee the independence of Faenza. And in the same fatal year in Bologna, one of the great families, the Malvezzi, laid its plans for the extinction of the other, the Bentovoglio, who were to be killed on a November evening as they sat at supper in their splendid palace. However, through the carelessness of one of the conspirators, the plot

Anonymous bust of king Charles VIII.

Lorenzo the Magnificent at the Conference of Cremona.

was discovered and arrests and vengeance followed for those of the Malvezzi who could not manage to escape to a friendly Milan. Lorenzo, appealed to by both sides refused to interfere. 'He consented and he did not consent' as one of the Malvezzi reported.

During 1490 and 1491, Lorenzo was harassed by the quarrel between

Fresco by Giorgio Vasari.

Ferrante and Innocent, which was the more dangerous because Innocent threatened to take up his residence in France: 'If none will aid Us against the violence of the King of Naples, We shall betake Ourselves abroad where We shall be received with great enthusiasm. We cannot remain in Italy if We are deprived of the dignity befitting the Vicar of Christ . . . ' Lorenzo, however,

Lorenzo receives the representatives of the town of Sarzana.

continued to arbitrate and argue and in the February of 1492 – only a few weeks before his death – he was successful in bringing them to a mutual understanding.

In twenty-two years Lorenzo had perfected what his grandfather, Cosmo *Pater Patriae*, had initiated and created between Florence, Naples, Milan, Venice and the Papal States, a firm balance of power which, as long as his influence watched over it, could keep Italy at peace. And he had done more than that. In place of the chronic enmity with her neighbours which had

Fresco by Giorgio Vasari.

hitherto always been Florence's lot, he slowly substituted friendly relations
with Siena, Lucca, Bologna, Faenza, Rimini, Perugia, and Città di Castello,
and so encircled Florence with a ring of friendly states – a more practical
guarantee of peace than even a general balance of power.

More importantly in the ultimate scale of values he made Florence the
teacher of Italy. On books alone he spent annually a sum whose modern
equivalent would be in excess of a million pounds. He twice sent an emissary
to the East for the express purpose of discovering and purchasing ancient

231

manuscripts and, on one of these visits, procured over two hundred Greek works, eighty of which up to that time were unknown. But this was only one item in his expenditure. Copies of the manuscripts had to be multiplied for general use and Lorenzo maintained an army of copyists, kept continuously at work.

Then, again, there were colleges to be founded for the assistance of those who had the scholar's instinct but could not afford the necessary books. Lorenzo's liberality to the University of Pisa, which he founded when he was twenty-three (at the time, incidentally, when he and Giuliano were chiefly renowned for their famous pageants and other festivities, including horse-races through the city's streets and squares), made it the most famous university of the time in Europe except that of Florence itself. While the University of Pisa was 'for the study of the Latin language and those branches of science of which it was the principal vehicle', it was at Florence only in all Italy that the Greek language was taught 'by which the knowledge of the Greek was extended not only through all the rest of Italy, but through France, Spain, Germany and England, from all which countries numerous students attended at Florence who diffused the learning they had there acquired through Europe'. The first two English Professors of Greek – William Grocyn and Thomas Linacre – acquired their knowledge at Florence under the great scholars Johannes Argyropolous and Demetrius Chalcondylas whom Lorenzo had provided.

And perhaps the greatest tribute to Lorenzo the Magnificent was that he died a much poorer man than his father or his grandfather and that his dying words to Poliziano and Pico della Mirandola, as they stood weeping by his bed, were, 'I wish that Death had spared me till I had completed your libraries.'

The medal of Marsilio Ficino.

The Shadow of Savonarola

The Florentine Renaissance had produced its own saint – Antonio Perozzi who died as Archbishop of Florence when Lorenzo was ten and a century later was raised to the altars of the Church as St Antoninus, with his feast day on May 10. (He is the only Antoninus in the Calendar for, though christened Antonio the diminutive 'Antonino' had clung to him from his earliest years on account of his small stature and his gentle disposition.)

At the age of fifteen, Antonino was the first postulant to take the Dominican habit at their new house at Fiesole and in 1436 he founded the great new house of San Marco in Florence, which his friend and fellow friar, Fra Angelico, decorated and for which Cosmo de' Medici so splendidly rebuilt the adjacent church. Of Cosmo's own cell in San Marco mention has already been made and an inscription over the entrance records that he had it built so that he might converse in greater privacy with Antonino and Fra Angelico. Cosmo had so little doubt of Antonino's sanctity that he publicly asserted that the preservation of Florence from the many dangers that threatened it was largely due to the merits and prayers of its holy Archbishop.

As Archbishop, Antonino continued to observe the holy poverty to which he was bound by his vows as a Dominican. His household consisted of six persons only; he kept no horses and even the one mule which served the needs of the establishment was often sold to assist the needs of the poor, though it was always bought back by some wealthy citizen and restored to its charitable owner. The Archbishop insisted on visiting the whole of his diocese once a year on foot and gave audience daily to all comers. His reputation for wisdom and integrity was such that his advice was asked continually by those in authority, lay as well as ecclesiastical, and when Pope Eugenius IV knew that he was dying, he summoned Antonino to Rome that he might receive from him the last sacraments and die in his arms.

Antonino, as befitted the child of the Florentine springtime of learning, was a profound scholar and the European authority on Canon Law. But the

233

appellation he most cherished was 'Protector of the Poor', an unofficial post he filled in the most intelligent way of establishing a company of twelve pious and wealthy citizens to give secret help to the unfortunate who were ashamed to beg. They were associated with the tiny church of San Martino which was made into a depository for gifts and contributions and the members were known as the *Buonuonimi di San Martino* – the good men of St Martin, the saint who shared his cloak with a beggar.

Antonino died five years before Cosmo and the presence of the *Pater Patriae* combined with the remembrance of the saint kept the fame and importance of San Marco alive during Lorenzo's early years. During the years of his own rule however the quality of the Dominicans declined and the two hundred and fifty or so brethren shrank to less than fifty. Partly this was the result of the expanding classical knowledge and the informed interest in comparative religion. The artists led the way and Botticelli's Blessed Virgins had an unmistakable facial affinity with his Aphrodites which might be easily explained by the philosophers who attended the debates of the Platonic Academy, who discussed also how far Eros was a God of Death as well as of Love.

The fact that it was St Augustine (who, before his conversion, was a Neo-Platonist and after it continued meditating on much the same lines if now with a Christian emphasis) who had in his *De Trinitate* propounded the idea of the 'pagan vestiges of the Trinity', was in itself almost sufficient to ensure that Lorenzo's patronage went to the Augustinians. For the General of that order, Fra Mariano da Genazzano, he restored in great splendour the church and monastery of Santo Spirito, the Augustinian headquarters in Florence which had been so disastrously damaged by the fire at the time of the Duke of Milan's visit during the Easter of 1471. A new church was designed by Brunelleschi and, though the architect himself died, erected in partial conformity with his plans so that the completion of the dome in 1482 ensured that the new church could be taken into use, and the remains of the old buildings demolished. On the site of them a new sacristy was built to the design of one of Lorenzo's favourite architects who had already designed a magnificent monastery for Mariano and a hundred Augustinians near the San Gallo Gate.

The architect's name was Giuliano Giamberti. In the dark days of 1478, when the resistance of Colle saved Florence, Lorenzo had sent him to Castellina, about eight miles from Colle. As Vasari tells the story: 'Lorenzo being obliged to send an engineer to Castellina to make bastions and direct

Opposite: *'Antonino' Perozzi, the founder of the great new house of San Marco: drawing attributed to Fra Bartolomeo.*

their artillery, a thing then understood by few, dispatched Giuliano as being the best fitted and the most dexterous and quick, knowing him to be, as the son of Francesco Giamberti, devoted to the Medici house. When Giuliano reached Castellina he fortified it within and without with good walls, bastions and other necessary things for defensive works. Perceiving the men to be slow and timid in manoeuvring the artillery, he turned his attention to this, and from that time no accidents occurred, whereas many had previously lost their lives through ignorance of their duties. Giuliano thereupon took charge of the artillery and his skill in firing and making use of it became so great and he so terrified the enemy that they soon came to terms and departed. For this, Giuliano won no small praise from Lorenzo at Florence, where he was ever afterwards in great favour.'

When Lorenzo decided to build a new house for Mariano and his Augustinians near the Porta San Gallo, many artists prepared models but it was that of the practical-minded artilleryman which was chosen and, from that moment, he became generally known as Giuliano da San Gallo. To Lorenzo the new house stood for something very near to his heart, for not only was Mariano his friend, but there met regularly there a company almost challenging comparison with the Platonic Academy. The 'da San Gallo' was indeed an appellation of honour, though at first the artist resented it.

'One day', Vasari records, 'he said jestingly to Lorenzo: "It is your fault in calling me 'da San Gallo' that I have lost my ancient family name, and so while I was flattering myself on my progress due to my ancient stock, I am going backwards!" Lorenzo retorted that he ought rather to desire to be the founder of a new house through his own abilities than to be dependent on others; and so Giuliano Giamberti was satisfied.'

Of the company which met at the new San Gallo house where an Augustinian revival of Christian mysticism combined with a formal cult of Cicero and Virgil, Poliziano has left an account: 'I have met Fra Mariano repeatedly at the villa and entered into confidential talks with him. I never knew a man at once more attractive and more cautious. He neither repels by immoderate severity nor deceives and leads astray by exaggerated indulgence. Many preachers think themselves masters of men's life and death. While they are abusing their power, they always look gloomy and weary men by setting up as judges of morals. But here is a man of moderation. In the pulpit he is a severe censor; but when he descends from it he indulges in winning, friendly

Opposite: *Giuliano Giamberti, who was later nick-named Giuliano da San Gallo after his successful design for a new house for the Augustinians near the Porta San Gallo : portrait by Piero di Cosimo.*

Robert Mitchum? 237

Above: *Savonarola preaching: frontispiece of his* Compendio di Rivelazione, *published in 1495.*

Opposite: *Antonino preaching in the church of San Marco: bas-relief by Fra Domenico Partigiani.*

discourse. Therefore I and my friend Pico [della Mirandola] have much conversation with him and nothing refreshes us after our literary labours as relaxation in his company. Lorenzo de' Medici, who understands men so well, shows how highly he esteems him, not only in that he has built him a splendid monastery, but also in that he often visits him, preferring a conversation with him to any other recreation.'

This new convent had a life of less than twenty years, for when after Lorenzo's death the Medici were driven from Florence it was razed to the ground by the same democratic mobs who plundered the Palazzo Medici and pillaged and destroyed all that Lorenzo and his father and his grandfather had managed to collect to make Florence the possessor of the greatest treasure-house of the arts in the world.

Not a trace is left of the San Gallo monastery which, for a few years, became the intellectual and spiritual centre of the city when Lorenzo and Fra Mariano and Angelo Poliziano and Pico della Mirandola and their chosen friends including the young Michelangelo met in the new library which *Il Magnifico* had provided to discuss philosophy and theology. Its place is occupied by the rows of trees and groves known as The Parterre.

This lack of a building has had a curious result in causing an imbalance in the popular view of Florentine history. Had the San Gallo monastery – or even the ruins of it – survived, the true course of events would be easier to see. The shift of importance of San Marco and the Dominicans under Cosmo to Santo Spirito and the Augustinians under Lorenzo would be clearly marked and the appointment of Fra Girolamo Savonarola as the new Prior of San Marco in 1491 seen not, as it is usually represented, as a continuation of Dominican greatness but as it was, as a challenge to Augustinian supremacy.

Girolamo Savonarola, three years younger than Lorenzo, was born in 1453 in Ferrara where his grandfather was a physician at the brilliant court of the Dukes of Este. The boy was precocious and much influenced by his grandfather whose hobby was the writing of ascetical tracts. Girolamo, one of a family of six, was a solitary and melancholy boy, who devoted himself to theology and in a poem entitled *The Ruin of the World* expressed adequately enough his basic concerns: 'Into the hands of a pirate the sceptre of Rome is fallen and St Peter is crushed to the ground. Vice and plunder there abound. So much so that I cannot conceive why Heaven itself is not troubled. So heavy with vice is the earth that it cannot rise from its oppression. The days of piety and purity are past. Virtue goes begging, never to walk again. But well I know that when it comes to the next life we shall see whose soul is the fairest, whose wings fly in the better style!'

Eventually he ran away from home to join the Dominicans at Bologna leaving behind him a lengthy tract entitled *Contempt for the World* for his parents' edification and a long letter to his father saying: 'My honoured Father, I cannot doubt about how you feel about my going away, especially as I left secretly. That is why I want you to realise what is in my mind and purpose. I have not behaved as a child as some people believe. But first what I want from you is to be strong enough and sufficiently able to despise the passing things of the world to follow the way of truth. You must reasonably judge my decision to flee the world and follow my resolve. The reason I have decided to enter religion is this: first, the great misery of the world, the iniquities of men, the rapes, the adulteries, the pride, the idolatry, the cruel

Opposite: *Girolamo Savonarola, the Dominican friar who made himself dictator of Florence after Lorenzo's death: detail of a fresco by Raphael.*

blasphemies. I cannot bear the great malice of Italy's blinded people, the more so as I see virtue utterly withering away and vice mounting. This causes me the greatest suffering I can experience in this world. Tell me – is there not much more merit in a man fleeing from the filth and evils of the miserable world so as to live like a rational being than like a beast among swine? So, my sweetest father, you have greater reason to thank the Lord Jesus Christ than to complain. He has made your son into a soldierly knight. Do you not feel it a great grace to have a son a knight of Jesus Christ.'

The self-revelation of this 'priggish and pretentious letter' (as Count Michael de la Bedoyère calls it in his life of the preacher) is confirmed by a subsequent letter to his mother: 'I know you are wondering why I have not written to you for so many days, but there have been no messengers. It is true that one of our friars was on the way to Ferrara after Christmas, but I was so busy that I quite forgot to write.' And later, in a letter of condolence on the death of her brother, he tells her 'these deaths of ours should teach us not to accumulate wealth, not to live in fine style, not to dress grandly. I pray therefore that you and my sisters give yourselves over to solitude, spiritual reading and prayer. Do not worry about society whether you see people or they see you . . . and you, my mother, I pray that you will forget this world.'

Thereupon he retails the story of the recent deaths of 'a young, fresh and healthy young man and of a young singing-girl, the most popular in Bologna' who was painfully struck down in child-birth 'carrying the punishment of her sins'. He adds: 'Perhaps if she had followed the way of life I once explained to you she might not have come to such a pass.'

The sex-obsessed egomaniac who, in the name of God, was to bring Florence to ruin, gained quick promotion among the Dominicans at Bologna and within seven years held the responsible post of Novice-Master. But, emerging raw from the cloister, he was sent on missions round northern Italy and, in Florence at least, was a complete failure. When he visited the city in 1483 to preach the Lenten sermons at San Lorenzo, his congregations were extremely small and the reception accorded to him by a city which had known the genuine sanctity of St Antoninus and enjoyed still the eloquence, tact and learning of Fra Mariano ('God's angel on earth' according to the consuls of Norcia who begged Lorenzo to allow him to visit them) was one of derision for his crudities of matter and manner. It was no wonder that Fra Mariano was filling the Duomo, while, at San Lorenzo, Savonarola could attract no more than twenty-five women and children.

Opposite: *Girolamo Savonarola's own cell in the Friary of San Marco, from which he used to peer discourteously when Lorenzo was walking in the garden.*

Savonarola's failure in Florence inevitably, for one of his temperament, bred hatred of the city. 'I cannot live unless I preach', he said, and during the next six years he travelled from town to town perfecting his oratory as an instrument of revolution. Eventually in Brescia in 1485 in a series of sermons on the Apocalypse, threatening the destruction of the wicked Church and pleasure-loving states, he came, oratorically speaking, of age. He prophesied that in a few years the Church would be scourged and, afterwards, renewed. In the beginning, he denied that this was a special revelation from God and that it was the conclusion which all could draw from a careful study of the Old Testament and the apocalyptic vision of St John, but gradually, as he savoured the popularity his diatribes brought him, he made greater claims and changed his general denunciations based on analogies between past and present to particular prophecies of the deaths shortly of Pope Innocent VIII, Ferrante of Naples and Lorenzo de' Medici.

Savonarola seems genuinely to have possessed to some degree at least the gift of second-sight. This led to his interest in and reputation for magic which in fact brought about his return to the city that has spurned him. He expressed it: 'God, having made choice of me, His unworthy and unprofitable servant, caused me to go to Florence by order of my superiors in the year 1489. In this year on August 1, I began publicly to expound the Apocalypse in the Church of San Marco.'

The will of the Almighty in this instance, as intrepreted by Savonarola's superiors, was Lorenzo de' Medici's request to them, on behalf of Pico della Mirandola, that Savonarola might be sent to Florence; and the superiors, in consideration of the connection of San Marco with the Medici and of Lorenzo's continuing benefactions to it, Santo Spirito notwithstanding, made haste to oblige him.

Pico's theses on the synthesis of all religions had been understandably rejected by Innocent VIII, but the young man insisted on replying. He defended thirteen of the more important propositions and accused the Vatican judges of heresy, implying in his preface that the execrable Latin in which their decision was announced suggested that their scholarship was of so low an order that they probably did not understand what he was writing about. The 'stammering barbarians' replied – in the persons of two bishops with inquisitorial powers – by interdicting the printing of the theses and having Pico excommunicated.

Pico fled to France, but he was arrested at the behest of the Roman

Opposite: *Frontispiece of a book of songs published in Florence: Savonarola preached against every aspect of the decadent sport and luxury to which he considered the city to be committed.*

Nuncio and confined for a while in a dungeon at Vincennes, until, by the intervention of Lorenzo, he was allowed to return to Florence. His excommunication was not rescinded; such a possibility indeed was not even considered, since Innocent VIII's bull *Summis desiderantes* against sorcery and witchcraft, promulgated in 1484, had been constructed on the narrowest of principles enunciated by the *Malleus Maleficarum*.

This treatise was the work of two Dominicans, James Sprenger, the Provincial of the Order and Inquisitor-General for Germany, and a younger Swiss colleague, Henry Kramer. Possibly they knew well their fellow Dominican at Bologna and certainly Savonarola studied the same sources of occult knowledge which they had to investigate. Thus Pico might well imagine that the much-acclaimed preacher would have a deeper understanding of the points at issue than had the authors of *The Witches' Hammer*, more especially as in his writings he had shown some affinity with Neo-Platonism. Savonarola's dialogue *De veritate prophetica*, for instance, not only opened in a pseudo-Socratic tone of doubt and introduced, in the names of the questioners, some of the Hebrew acrostics which were dear to Pico, but the setting of the conversation was one which the Platonic Academy was accustomed to use – the inspiring plane tree on the bank of the Ilissus, under which Socrates invited Phaedrus to sit, reappearing as a plane tree on the outskirts of Florence.

But it soon became apparent that the only prophecies in the truth of which Savonarola was interested were the threats of the blood-thirsty Jehovah of the Old Testament. To the friar's temperament, the gracious ambience of Greece was anathema and he soon gave full rein to his denunciations: 'Heed my warnings, you who are rich and powerful, for your punishment will come. Florence shall no longer be a city of flowers. It will be called a den of thieves, of vice and of blood.'

It was for Lorenzo himself that Savonarola reserved his bitterest invective and persistent discourtesy. After his preaching, fortified by prophecy, had at last won the crowds to listen to him and thus provided him with popular backing, his egoism so increased that he showed clearly the symptoms of his spiritual disease by repudiating any authority but God's voice to him personally. His election as Prior of San Marco in the summer of 1491 made these imaginings the easier and on this occasion he refused to pay the conventional visit which, from the days of Cosmo and St Antonino, the new Prior, out of courtesy, was accustomed to pay to the head of the Medici family to whose generosity San Marco owed so much. 'I hold my election from God alone,' said Savonarola 'and to Him alone I owe obedience!'

The new Prior also took the precaution of leaving the garden of San Marco whenever Lorenzo made a visit to it and sending the message, should Lorenzo

Savonarola's medal: on the verso is portrayed the doom which he continually prophesied for Florence.

wish to speak with him, that his conversation was not with man but with God.

Lorenzo with a wry smile remarked, 'A stranger has come into my house and will not deign even to visit me.' But he sent the usual gifts and money to San Marco and was sufficiently courteous, when in that garden which as a boy he had helped to plant, not to notice Savonarola peeping at him through the window of his private room.

In his public discourses, whether sermons or political addresses Savonarola lost no opportunity of attacking the credit and diminishing the reputation of Lorenzo by predicting his early death and by accusing him of ruining Florence by his patronage of sport and luxury. On one occasion when he had overstepped all bounds of decency, five prominent citizens of Florence went to San Marco to exhort him to moderation. He assumed that Lorenzo had sent them – which was not so – and told them to go back to him and bid him repent of his sins and to remember that God, in the vengeance that was looming, would spare no one. The deputation warned the friar that he could be exiled. Savonarola retorted that though Lorenzo was a Florentine citizen and he a stranger, Lorenzo would leave Florence before he did and once more he prophesied his early death as a thing specially revealed to him.

There was, though, little need for special revelation to make such a prognostication. By the beginning of 1491, Lorenzo's hereditary gout had infected his whole system. From his feet it had spread to every part of his body. The frequent water cures which he took mitigated the pain but produced no radical effect on the disease itself, which gained such a hold that during that year (1491) he lost for a time the use of his legs and was compelled to neglect much of his public business.

It was natural that, with the prospect of death continually before him, his life-long interest in religion should increase. One of his reiterated beliefs was: 'He is dead even to this life who has no hopes of another', and in the new Augustinian monastery he held frequent discussions with Fra Mariano and his other friends on the existence of the Deity, the insufficiency of temporal enjoyments to fill the mind and the certainty of the Resurrection of Christ as well as the moral necessity, philosophically, of a future state.

Fra Mariano who regarded Lorenzo as one of the most profound Christians he knew, felt it incumbent on him to do what he could to right the public balance and, on Ascension Day, he preached a great sermon on Christ's last words to His disciples before leaving them and ascending to Heaven: 'It is not for you to know the times and seasons which the Father hath put in His own power.' At the conclusion of a brilliant and learned exposition of the true nature of Scriptural prophecy, he accused the Prior of San Marco of being a false prophet, one of those 'seducers who shall wax worse and worse, both deceiving and being deceived' against whom the New Testament warned when it proclaimed that 'the time will come when they will not endure sound doctrine, but after their own likes shall take to themselves teachers, having itching ears.' And not only was Savonarola a false prophet but he was an instigator of sedition among the people, a stirrer-up of strife and disorder.

Lorenzo himself, in spite of the pleadings of his friends, would make no move against the insolent Dominican. He merely said that as long as the preacher exerted himself to reform the wicked of Florence he would readily excuse any incivility to himself. 'This extraordinary degree of lenity', comments Roscoe, perceptively, 'if it had no influence on the mind of the fanatic prevented in a great degree the ill effects of his harangues; and it was not till after the death of Lorenzo that Savonarola excited those disturbances in Florence which led to his own destruction and terminated in the ruin of the Republic.'

The proceedings and outlook of Savonarola had very little, if any, connection with Christianity. For him, 'sin' was 'sex'. He was the archetypal puritan who had no understanding of the religion of the Incarnation – the Fleshing of

Opposite: *Lorenzo's son Piero: portrait by Bronzino.*

Overleaf: *Savonarola had instituted his 'Bonfire of vanities' at carnival-time in the Piazza della Signoria. It was here that two of his fellow-heretics were, with himself, hanged, and their dead bodies burned in the May of 1498, as is shown in this painting by an anonymous artist.*

God – whose Founder was known in His lifetime as 'a gluttonous man and a winebibber', whose first public act was to turn water into wine and whose last to turn wine into His Blood and whose teaching included the maxim to take no thought for the morrow.

The hatred and fear of the body which characterises the ascetic was the hall-mark of the major heresy which the Christian Church had to fight from the beginning, and any suggestion that the 'flesh', which God had taken upon Himself for a lifetime and afterwards borne back to Heaven and enthroned in the Godhead Itself, could be intrinsically 'evil' pointed immediately to profound heresy with which the Church had had to battle since the second century. When the lives of those saints who had, for the sheer love of God, voluntarily sacrificed the keenest of human pleasures as a token of their love for Him, were being examined to determine whether or not their sanctity was genuine, any ascetic sympton which could be construed as contempt for the body was eagerly seized on by the Devil's Advocate in the canonisation process as *prima facie* evidence of heresy. (When, for example, at the murder of Thomas Becket, it was discovered that he wore a hair shirt, it was immediately assumed that he was the leader of an heretical cult.) In Savonarola's case, his heresy was clear enough and he was eventually condemned and executed for heresy and schism. His pride and self-identification with Christ become such that 'it was his habit to turn to the crucifix and say to Our Lord: "If I lie, you lie too." ' And to keep his reputation for supernatural knowledge, he had ensured that many friars of his order 'should hear confessions and report to him what they had learnt. And afterwards he inveighed against these reported sins both publicly in the pulpit and privately and pretended that he knew of them by revelation.'

Of his own sins, Savonarola admitted in 1498 that for fourteen years he had never made a genuine confession – a period which covered the whole of his time in Florence. This hindsight, though interesting, is hardly necessary. His conduct makes it probable enough.

Though it was not till after Lorenzo's death that Savonarola's hatred of life blazed into the Bonfire of Vanities, the clash between the two men centred, in practice, in their attitudes to the simple amusements of *l'homme moyen sensuel*. What Savonarola organised his gangs of youths (roughly speaking, the 'skin-heads' of the period) to destroy was the Carnival and everything of wit and joy and beauty and untrammelled sexual amusement associated with it. And the Carnival was the invention of Lorenzo.

Opposite: *Niccolo Mauruzi da Tolentino fighting in the battle of San Romano: detail from a painting by Paolo Uccello which hung in Lorenzo's bedroom in the Palazzo Medici.*

The Carnival (*carne vale*! – farewell to flesh) denoting the days immediately before Lent was a period of varying length, sometimes merely Shrove Tuesday (which was properly a synonym for it), sometimes the three weeks from Septuagesima to Shrove Tuesday which the Church calls 'the Porch of Lent', sometimes the whole period from the end of Epiphany to Ash Wednesday.

In Carnival time it was the custom of the Florentines to walk the streets masked and singing popular ballads. Lorenzo saw that here was an opportunity of delighting the people with magnificent pageantry. He caused the Triumphs (*Trionfi*) in which he took part to be prepared by his best artists and the mythological costumes of the episodes represented by the masquers to be researched by his scholars and the music entrusted to the best musicians. When the carts carried representatives of the arts and trades they were known by the simpler name of *Carri*. The lyrics written for the *Trionfi* were usually classical and stately, whereas those intended to be sung on the *Carri* were plebeian and popular and, to use J. A. Symonds's description, 'dealt in almost undisguised obscenity', Lorenzo wrote both, with equal skill and enjoyment and the publication of his Carnival Songs, *Canti Carnascialeschi*, after his death contained the information by Il Lasca, the editor that 'this Festival was invented by the Magnificent Lorenzo de' Medici.'

'It was their wont', Il Lasca explained, 'to go forth after dinner and often they lasted for three or four hours into the night, with a multitude of masked men on horseback following, richly dressed, exceeding sometimes three hundred in number and as many men on foot with lighted torches. Thus they traversed the city, singing to the accompaniment of music arranged for four, eight, twelve or even fifteen voices, supported by various instruments.'

Lorenzo's fancy took the Florentine mind. Carnival, in this sense, was repeated each year, as a kind of new festival to rival the great summer celebrations connected with the Feast of St John the Baptist. The finest artists and poets and musicians gave of their best to make them splendid, with Lorenzo himself and Poliziano writing verses at every level, from the highest to the coarsest. In the collection of songs for Carnival, there survive Masques of Scholars, Artisans, Frog-catchers, Furies, Tinkers, Grape-sellers, Old Men and Young Wives, Tortoiseshell Cats, Nymphs in love, Nuns escaped from their convents, Gypsies, Devils, Young Men who have lost their fathers, Jews, Lawyers, Perfumers and Damned Souls. 'The tone of these songs' – to quote again J. A. Symonds who was one of the earliest English experts on them – 'is uniformly and deliberately immoral. One might fancy them composed for some old phallic festival.'

Lorenzo's greatest contribution to the Carnival was his *Trionfo di Bacco e d'Arianna*, 'The Triumph of Bacchus and Ariadne', of which Titian's picture of that name (probably based on remembrance of a similar pageant car in

Titian's The Triumph of Bacchus and Ariadne.

Venice) gives a radiant hint with the characters – the cymbal-clashing Bac-
chantes, the little fauns and satyrs, the male devotees of the god, naked but
for a few vine-leaves, the struggling Silenus – who, dancing and singing,
would attend the chariot. Even the two leopards which – correctly – drew
the god's car may have originally appeared in Lorenzo's *Trionfo*.

And the song he provided, *Quant' è bella giovanezza*, is certainly his most
famous. (It was appropriated by the Fascists as their national anthem in the
1920s and altered for their purposes but in its original it was, as C. M. Ady says,
'the very essence of the Carnival as seen through Lorenzo's eyes'.) It runs –
in Symonds's translation:

255

Fair is youth and void of sorrow
But it hourly flies away –
Youths and maids, enjoy today;
Naught ye know about tomorrow

This is Bacchus and the bright
Ariadne, lovers true!
They, in flying time's despite,
Each with each find pleasure new;
These their Nymphs and all their crew
Keep perpetual holiday
Youths and maids enjoy today;
Naught ye know about tomorrow.

And so, for eight stanzas, the song continued, returning to the central theme –

Quant' è bella giovanezza
Che si fugge tuttavia!
Chi vuol esser lieto, sia;
Di doman non c'è certezza.

Such were the songs and sights which prompted Savonarola eventually to stage (after Lorenzo's death and during his own dictatorship) his counter to the Carnival. On Shrove Tuesday an immense fir tree was placed in the Piazza Signoria, with large boards lying on the many tiers of the flat green branches. At the heart of the pyramid, a keg of gunpowder was placed. The citizens of Florence had been exhorted by the friar and by the hordes of youths, better organised than ever, to place their 'vanities' – or to give them to the children to place – on the shelves. 'Vanities' meant not only women's finery, make-up, powders and false hair and men's cards, dice and other means of gambling secured by the youthful militia using their sticks of office with the permission of the *Signoria* to use them, but volumes of Petrarch and Boccaccio as well as classical authors, musical instruments and tapestries and exquisite paintings in which nudity occurred and jewels and gay frivolous masquing clothes. All through Shrove Tuesday, boys in white dressed as angels and garlanded with olive superintended the preparations and, when at nightfall the trumpets sounded and the gunpowder was set off to cause a spectacle out-carnivalling Carnival, they sang what were considered appropriate hymns.

Opposite: *The statue of Bacchus made by the young Michelangelo when under the influence of the Platonic Academy. It immediately preceded his famous* Piéta *in St Peter's, Rome.*

Illustration of Bacchus and Ariadne, the subject of one of Lorenzo's carnivals in Florence : anonymous engraving of the fifteenth century.

The true irony of the situation lies in the fact that they could have been – though Savonarola sàw to it that they were not – Lorenzo's hymns. For he, the full man, experiencing and rejoicing in the fullness of life at every level, wrote *laudi* for the people to sing as well as *canti*. After Carnival came Lent, to which no hymn was more appropriate than his lovely *Poich' io gustai, Gesù, la tua dolcezze* – 'Since I have tasted, Jesus, all Thy sweetness' in which he sings of His loving-kindness, who

> Didst deign to die that we, Thy sons, might live,
>   To be a man that I might be divine;
> Didst not refuse to make Thyself a slave,
>   That I might not be bond, nor live in vain.

> (*Che per dar vita à 'Figli à te dai morte,*
>   *E per farmi divin se' fatto umano*
> *Preso hai di servo condizione e sorte,*
>   *Perch' io servo non sia, o vivo in vano.*)

In another of his hymns, Lorenzo chides his own hard and malignant heart

258

'fount of every evil imagining'. Yet another is the supplication of a sinner for God's mercy.

Quite apart from his particular obsessions, Savonarola could not be expected to understand Lorenzo's simple orthodoxy – when he did at last visit him on his deathbed his first question was to enquire whether he was a Christian – but the use to which the friar put Lorenzo's Carnival activities was unnecessarily grotesque. He denounced them from the pulpit as being a deliberate attempt to debauch the citizens so that he could more easily tyrannise over them. 'The tyrant', he said, 'in times of peace and plenty, is wont to occupy the people with shows and festivals in order that they may think of their own pastimes and not of his designs so that, growing unused to the conduct of the commonwealth, they may leave the reins of government in his hands.'

Whether Savonarola really believed this, it is difficult to tell. No one in Florence was likely to take any notice of it and the Senate's description of Lorenzo on his death as one who 'subordinated his personal interest to the advantage and benefit of the community and shrank from neither trouble nor dangers for the good of the Republic and its freedom', hardly suggests a deliberate policy of enervation, which, in itself, is sufficiently absurd. But it was good enough for foreigners and, most unfortunately, has tainted the judgment of posterity which, in the hands of 'liberal' historians and Protestant enthusiasts who see Savonarola as the precursor of Luther in his denunciation of the Pope, see Lorenzo through Savonarola's eyes. Thus at the beginning of the nineteenth century, Sismondi in his monumental history of the Italian republics, set the fashion for a century or more when he wrote: 'Lorenzo was a bad citizen of Florence as well as a bad Italian; he degraded the character of the Florentines, destroyed their energy, ravished from them their liberty. He confirmed in Florence the taste for pleasure and luxury as a means of confirming his power.'

So has the shadow of Savonarola unfortunately fallen across history, obscuring and distorting the truth.

The Death of Lorenzo

Guicciardini objectively described Florence on the eve of Lorenzo's death: 'The city was in perfect peace. The citizens in whose hands was the administration held firmly together; the government, carried on and supported by them, was so powerful that no one dared contradict it. The people were daily entertained with festivals, spectacles and novelties; the city abounded in everything; trades and business were at the height of prosperity. Men of talent found their proper place in the great liberality with which the arts and sciences were promoted and those who practised them were honoured. This city, quiet and peaceful at home, enjoyed high esteem and great consideration abroad, because she had a government whose head had full authority; because her dominions had lately been extended; because she had complete sway over Pope Innocent; and because, in alliance with Naples and Milan, she in some measure kept Italy in equilibrium.'

It would, however, be entirely wrong to suppose that there were not occasions for tensions between Lorenzo and his fellow citizens. They were inevitabilities arising from the anomalous financial situation. The strikings of the balance between what he owed the State and what the State owed him was difficult enough, but if it be conceded that he may have sometimes cast the account too much in his own favour (in the war of the Pazzi conspiracy, for instance, his bank charged eight per cent commission for paying the troops instead of the customary seven per cent) the fact remained that he so ordered matters when peace was restored that in 1492 direct taxation had been cut back to the level of 1470.

The two points which affected the public at large and earned Lorenzo a certain amount of unpopularity were the debasement of coinage and the rearrangement of the Dowry Fund, the *Monti delle Doti*. In the summer of 1490 a new committee, of which Lorenzo was a member, was set up to deal with finance. Its first measure concerned the coinage. The Republic was overwhelmed with small and base foreign coins – Lucchese, Bolognese,

Sienese and others. It was very difficult to distinguish these *quattrini* from the Florentine which, outwardly, were very like them. On May 1, 1491, these 'black *quattrini*', as the foreign coins were called, were replaced by a new coin, containing two ounces of silver to a pound of copper, and reckoned as equivalent to five *danari* while the old one was called in at the rate of four *danari*. The public treasuries were to receive only the new 'white *quattrini*'. The people were pleased enough, until it was discovered that the old money, instead of being melted down, was stealthily brought into circulation and the old *quattrino* remained in use side by side with the new one. Out of the confusion, endless difficulties arose affecting everyone, for the people found that in paying taxes, duties, purchases of salt, everything where produce went into the treasury, they were the chief sufferers. Anticipating 'Gresham's Law' that 'bad money drives out good', they found the 'white' coins were driven into the hands of the already-too-wealthy bankers.

Even more exasperating was the matter of the Dowry Fund. The *Monte delle Doti* had been established in Cosmo de' Medici's day, in 1424, as a State Deposit bank. The creditors of the State were allotted shares in it to the extent of their claims, a portion of the shares being regarded as a State Insurance for securing dowries for the sons and daughters of the holders. The scheme was successful enough to be extended to any person willing to pay the required premium. In 1468, sons were excluded from the benefits of the fund, which was thereafter reserved for daughters only. The insurer might put down a lump sum or, if he wished, renew his premium annually. At the end of an agreed term of years, a dowry corresponding to the contribution was paid or the sum might be left in the hands of the bank at five per cent interest.

In 1485 a change of system was introduced. Only one-fifth of the total sum was to be paid in cash; the other four-fifths were to remain in the hands of the *Monte*, bearing seven per cent interest. In 1491 the new finance committee reduced this to three per cent.

As the majority of Florentines held stock in the *Monte* and for three generations had been accustomed to look forward to a full cash repayment after the agreed time, there was a general feeling of having been cheated when only a fifth of their legitimate expectations was realisable in cash. It was thus easy enough for Savonarola to canalise the general discontent by accusing Lorenzo of stealing the dowries of poor girls to line his own pocket. Since Lorenzo gained nothing whatever from what was after all only a readjustment by the State in its own interest of the affairs of a State Insurance Office, it was ridiculously far from the truth; but at the same time Lorenzo cannot escape some responsibility for a measure which, however theoretically sound (in that it benefited all who did not hold stock in the *Monte* as well as, by the conversion of redeemable into partially irredeemable securities, enhancing the public credit) was a grave social and financial disaster.

In extenuation it may be said that, for the last year of his life, he was so continuously ill that he was in no fit state for business of any kind. His gout alone was a great drawback as early as 1489, when he wrote to one of his correspondents in Rome: 'Pain in my feet has hindered my correspondence. Feet and tongue are indeed far apart, yet they interfere with each other!' To this were added the pains of arthritis and he could get rest neither day nor night. During 1491 he was attacked by a slow fever, which, in Poliziano's words, 'ate away the whole man, attacking not only the arteries and veins, but the limbs, intestines, nerves, bones and marrow'.

At the beginning of 1492, Lorenzo could see no one; all important political business had to be set aside; the Milanese ambassador waited a fortnight for an audience; the physicians were at their wits' end, but insisted that the illness was not mortal. His favourite doctor, Piero Leoni, warned him to avoid cold or damp feet and the air at sunset and enjoined him not to eat pears or swallow grape-pips. A visiting specialist, Lazaro of Pavia, who had been specially sent by Ludovico *Il Moro*, prepared a draught of pulverised pearls, diamonds and other costly substances. Lorenzo took their medicines, ate what they prescribed and, on being asked how it tasted, said: 'As it usually tastes to a dying man.' He seemed more concerned to soothe their feelings than to alleviate his own suffering and, according to Poliziano, noted their assiduity as they hovered round the bed 'so that they might appear to be doing something'. On the morning of Lorenzo's death, Piero Leoni committed suicide by drowning himself in a well.

It was on March 21, 1492, after rallying sufficiently to write that last great letter to his son, Giovanni, in Rome and saying to the messenger who carried it, 'You will not see me again', that Lorenzo left Florence for the last time to go to his villa at Careggi, where his father and his grandfather had died. 'The illustrious Lorenzo', wrote the Ferrarese ambassador, 'suffers so acutely that it is hard to understand how he can hold out. The doctors, indeed, do not consider the illness mortal; but his condition is getting very bad because he is so tormented with pain that he gets very little rest.'

With him were his sister, Bianca, his daughter, Lucrezia, and his 'Angel', Poliziano, who remained constantly with him. It was Bianca to whom fell the duty of telling him that he was dying. 'Brother', she said, 'you have lived great-mindedly and you must leave life bravely and piously. Know, then, that there is no hope left.'

'If it be God's will,' said Lorenzo, 'nothing can be pleasanter to me than death.'

He sent for his confessor and was given absolution and viaticum. Immedia-

Portrait of Lorenzo the Magnificent : fifteenth-century cameo in agate and onyx attributed to either Domenico Milanese or Giovanni delle Corniole.

tely afterwards, he spoke to his eldest son, Pietro, alone. According to Pietro's later account to Poliziano, the dying man said: 'The citizens, my Pietro, will undoubtedly recognise you as my successor and I do not doubt that you will obtain the same authority as I myself have had. But, as the commonwealth is a body with many heads and it is impossible to please them all, remember always to follow the course which appears the most honourable and always study the good of all rather than individual and particular interests.' He instructed Pietro to act as a father to the youngest boy, Giuliano, who was thirteen, and to see that Giovanni, the Cardinal, took an interest in the career of Giulio, the elder Giuliano's son, who was now fourteen and had been brought up as one of the family. (It seems that Lorenzo had already decided on an ecclesiastical career for his nephew and Giovanni, when he became Pope Leo X, certainly fulfilled his imposed duty to Giulio, who became Pope Clement VII.) Finally, Lorenzo impressed on Pietro the necessity for a simple funeral. There must be no ostentation or display, but the pattern of Cosmo's funeral should be followed and the limits usual for a private citizen's burial not be overstepped.

When the others returned to the room, their grief was such that, according to Poliziano, 'you might have thought each one of us was doomed to die except Lorenzo.' Angelo himself, because the nearest in love, was the most affected. When Lorenzo held out his arms to him and seized both hands in the strongest grasp of which he was capable, Poliziano turned his face away to hide his tears; and Lorenzo, realising his emotion, gradually relaxed his grasp and Angelo rushed to his own rooms to let his grief take its course.

As soon as he came back, Lorenzo asked why Pico did not come to see him. Poliziano answered that probably Pico feared to trouble him. Lorenzo replied that he rather feared it was the distance of the villa from the city that troubled Pico. Thus summoned, della Mirandola came at great speed to Careggi. Lorenzo, greeting him with affection, apologised for troubling him but asked him to regard it as a proof of his affection, because he would die more content after having seen him once more. Then they spoke of many things until Lorenzo's voice became so weak that they could scarcely hear him and for his sake had to abandon the conversation.

Last of all, after Pico had gone, came 'the haughty Savonarola, who probably thought that in the last moments of agitation and suffering he might be enabled to collect material for his factious purposes'.

So Roscoe described it and, in doing so, gets, I think, near the truth of that final meeting. For with Savonarola's intrusion there came several crucial

Opposite: *Allegory of the death of Lorenzo the Magnificent : fresco by Francesco Furini.*

questions. According to Poliziano, Savonarola exhorted the dying man to believe the Christian Faith, to amend his life, if it were spared to him, and, if it were not, to meet death with fortitude. He then read the prayers for the dying, to which Lorenzo made the responses, and gave him his blessing.

Poliziano's account of the death is supplemented but not contradicted by two others, by the chronicle of Cerretani, written from day to day, who adds the detail that at one point Lorenzo fainted with the pain and that a Camaldulensian friar gained assurance that he was not dead only by taking off his spectacles and holding them to the dying man's mouth. The other account was in a letter written by Benedetto Dei to a friend less than a week after the event: 'He died so nobly, with all the patience, the reverence, the recognition of God, which the best of holy men and a soul divine could show, with words upon his lips so kind that he seemed a new St Jerome.' He then repeats substantially Poliziano's account of how Lorenzo asked for the Gospel of the day – it was Passion Sunday – to be read to him, signifying by the movement of his lips that he was following it. When through exhaustion he could no longer do this, he raised his eyes from time to time or worked his fingers as a sign that he was still conscious. At last a silver crucifix was held close to his face. He kissed it with all his remaining strength and so died.

Savonarola's account of the deathbed, which he imparted to his two principal lieutenants, Fra Silvestro and Fra Domenico (who in their turn informed his biographers, so that, after the deaths of Lorenzo and Savonarola, it became the official version, endlessly repeated by historians), was very different. According to this, Lorenzo was so troubled in conscience that he sent for the friar as the holiest man in Florence to absolve him. The three things which troubled him were his responsibilities for the sack of Volterra, for the alteration in the Dower Fund and for the punishment of the Pazzi conspirators. To gain absolution, Lorenzo must do three things. He must have faith in God, he must restore what he had wrongfully appropriated and he must give back to the people of Florence the liberty he had deprived them of.

At this last demand, Lorenzo turned his back on him and the friar left the room, leaving him unabsolved. After a few hours he died, unshriven, screaming at the prospect of Hell and tortured by the realisation of sin unforgiven.

The complete falsity of the story is self-evident. In the first place, Lorenzo had already made his confession and been absolved, so that there was never any question of Savonarola giving him absolution. In the second place, none of the three subjects said to be troubling him could possibly be regarded as sins except for Savonarola's propaganda purposes. Lorenzo had done all he could to make what restitution was possible at Volterra; he had been

Opposite: *Death-mask of Lorenzo the Magnificent.*

noticeably, even dangerously, lenient to the Pazzi murderers and their accomplices; and the reorganisation of the *Monte* was, as he saw it, for the benefit of the State as a whole.

The question as to who falsified the interview, Savonarola or his disciples, is irrelevant. In the first place the version must have come from Savonarola, whose attitude it perfectly represents. The problem which many of us still find fascinating is how Savonarola came to be at the death-bed at all. Considering the relations between the two men, it is unlikely that Lorenzo or any of Lorenzo's friends invited him. As he appeared just after Pico della Mirandola, it is possible that he came, in fact, with him, on which account his presence would not be questioned even though he did not enter the bedroom till Pico had left it.

And his motive? There is nothing in the friar's conduct or character to contradict the suggestion that it was to cause Lorenzo pain – 'the friar was intransigent, arrogant and fanatical in the expression of his hatred and caused the ailing Lorenzo enormous suffering' as a French historian has it – but, in my opinion, the Dominican's motive was specifically to be in a position, as an eye-witness at the deathbed, to be able to authenticate his lie when the propaganda started to spread among the people. Also, he may have hoped to find Lorenzo dead and to be able to announce it as fulfilling his prophecy of the event.

When the news of the death reached Florence, the city was thrown into confusion. Signs and portents increased the tension. Three days before he died, a woman at Mass in Santa Maria Novella called out: 'Alas! citizens, do you not see the raging bull with flaming horns which is casting this temple to the ground?' Marsilio Ficino saw in his garden giant ghosts fighting each other and heard terrible and confused voices. Fiery lights blazed in the sky over the Villa Careggi and a star of unusual brightness illuminated the heavens while Lorenzo lay dying and disappeared at the moment of his death. The lantern of the Duomo was struck by lightning and some heavy blocks of marble were hurled down on the side toward the Palazzo Medici. Strangest of all, the lions in the Via di Leone fought each other so fiercely that some were killed – an unprecedented occurrence.

The assembled councils and citizens of Florence, in conjunction with the *Signoria*, issued the following decree: 'Whereas the foremost man of all this city, the lately deceased Lorenzo de' Medici, did, during his whole life, neglect no opportunity of protecting, increasing, adorning and raising this city, but was always ready with counsel, authority and painstaking, in thought and deed; subordinated his personal interest to the advantage and benefit of the community; shrank from neither trouble nor danger for the good of the

State and its freedom; and devoted to that object all his thoughts and powers, securing public order by excellent laws; by his presence brought a dangerous war to an end; regained the places lost in battle and took those belonging to the enemies; and whereas he furthermore, after the rare examples furnished by antiquity, for the safety of his fellow citizens and the freedom of his country gave himself up into his enemies' power and, filled with love for his house, averted the general danger by drawing it all on his own head; whereas, finally, he omitted nothing that could tend to raise our reputation and enlarge our borders; it has seemed good to the Senate and the people of Florence, on the motion of the chief magistrate, to establish a public testimonial of gratitude to the memory of such a man, in order that virtue might not be unhonoured among the Florentines, and that, in days to come, other citizens may be incited to serve the commonwealth with might and wisdom.'

It may pass for a just epitaph.

Michelangelo's *The Battle of the Centaurs.*

Afterword

Innocent III, on hearing of Lorenzo's death, exclaimed: 'The peace of Italy is at an end!' Four months later the Pope himself died, leaving only Ferrante of Naples – an old man now with no more than two years' life left to him – to face the flood from beyond the Alps that all Italy feared. Ferrante's verdict on Lorenzo's death had been: 'That man's life has been long enough for his own deathless fame, but too short for Italy. God grant that now he is dead that may not be attempted which was not ventured in his lifetime.' But everyone knew it was not to be. The dreaded French invasion was inevitable now that Lorenzo, the only man who could have averted it, was gone.

The quibbling excuses for the invasion – French rights in Naples – mattered neither then nor now. The mere fact was that King Louis XI of France, had left his successor, Charles VIII, a powerful standing army, the first there had ever been in Europe, with which to dominate the Continent whenever he wished.

Charles VIII, in the words of Rolfe (Corvo) which tallies with all historical records, 'was a self-conceited little abortion of the loosest morals even for a king, of gross semitic type, with a fiery birth-flare round his left eye, and twelve toes on his feet hidden in splayed shoes, which set the fashion in foot-gear for the end of the fifteenth century in Italy'. He crossed the Alps in the September of 1494 and was at the gates of Florence on November 17.

All that year, Savonarola preached on Noah's Ark and on Easter Day made an impassioned appeal to the Florentines to enter into the safety of the Ark; 'But a time will come when the Ark will be closed and many will then sorrow uselessly at not having entered into it.' Skilfully prolonging his analogy, he made the text 'Behold I will bring a flood of waters over the earth' coincide with the news that Charles had crossed the Alps, with his banners inscribed (at the suggestion of a wily cardinal who understood the propaganda-value of the friar's preaching that Charles was the new Cyrus, a scourge to punish the sinners of Florence, sent by God Himself), *Voluntas Dei* (God's Will),

Missus a Deo (Sent by God), and similar legends. The result was that, by the time the French had reached Sarzana, which Lorenzo had re-fortified as the guard of Florence, the Florentines were thoroughly demoralised by the reputation of the great, invincible force and its reputation for unspeakable atrocities. Even had Lorenzo's heir and successor, Pietro the Unfortunate, had any of his father's greatness, it would have been difficult to rally the Republic. But Pietro, who took after his mother, Clarice, and was additionally unpopular on account of his own wife, also an Orsini, was a greater disaster even than Savonarola.

He is known as *Lo Sfortuno*, but he was unfortunate only by his refusal to respond to his father's training. Lorenzo, by example and precept, had tried to make Pietro understand 'though you are my son, you are only a simple Florentine citizen like any other'. But Pietro and still less his wife made no effort to learn this first lesson of Florentine statecraft. The strain of Orsini arrogance which he inherited from his mother and which was encouraged by his Orsini wife, combined with a general frivolity, had made his father increasingly anxious about the headstrong and irresponsible youth who was so obviously unfitted to carry on the traditions of his house and who, as it happened, in two short years after *Il Magnifico's* death, brought it to ruin and exile.

Yet it might be argued that it was less his obvious vices which precipitated the ruin but a rather pathetic attempt to imitate his father. As Lorenzo had once saved Florence by giving himself into the power of an enemy, so Pietro would go alone into the French camp. However, as Guicciardini the historian, observed in recording the episode, it is dangerous to guide ourselves by precedent unless the cases be exactly alike; unless the attempt be conducted with equal prudence; and, above all, unless it be attended by the same good fortune. Pietro was quite unable to understand such distinctions. He threw himself at the feet of Charles VIII, who received his submission with coldness and disdain. Finding his entreaties useless, he became lavish in his promises to promote French interest, and, as a pledge of his fidelity, promised to deliver up to them not only the fortress of Sarzana, but also the towns of Pietra Santa and the cities of Pisa and Leghorn. When the news of such a betrayal reached Florence, the horrified *Signoria* decided to end Pietro's supremacy there and then pronounced a sentence of banishment and offered four thousand florins for his head and on his return to the city on November 9, 1494 he found the doors of the Signorial Palace shut against him and the people in the streets so passionately incensed that he thought it

Overleaf: *On Lorenzo's death, Charles VIII lost no time in marching his French army into Florence : painting by Francesco Granacci.*

wise to escape immediately and that night was riding over the Apennines to Bologna, never to see Florence again.

By permission of the *Signoria* the Medici palace was sacked by the mob aided by some of the French who were already in the city and urged on by the Savonarolists. Though Cardinal Giovanni, who was in Florence at the time, managed to save many of the most valuable manuscripts and refused to leave the city until he had deposited them in safety and though Pietro's wife managed to save some expensive curtains, Roscoe's judgment may be accepted: 'All that the assiduity and the riches of Lorenzo and his ancestors had been able to accumulate in half a century was dissipated or demolished in a day.'

The banishment of the Medici left it more easy for Savonarola to introduce Charles VIII as the Chosen of God (as there was little objective evidence that the King deserved the title, the friar affirmed it as a private revelation by the Deity to him personally) and on November 30, 1494, he entered the city in triumph. On the same day, Pico della Mirandola died.

Under Savonarola's influence, Florence became a titular theocracy. Christ was considered its King; a new coinage was struck with the Florentine *giglio* on one side and the inscription, *Senatus Populusque Florentinus*: and, on the other, a cross, with the affirmation, *Jesus Christus Rex Noster*; a new Great Council dominated by Savonarola's followers, the *Frateschi* (or *Piagnoni* – 'tear-jerkers' – as their opponents called them) was formed and in a sermon preached on December 14, 1494, the friar instructed the city: 'Place your trust nowhere but in the Great Council which is the work of God and not of men and may he who would change it be eternally cursed by God.'

After enduring Savonarola's increasing eccentricities for three years, Florence regained her sanity, while his heresies prompted an attack on him by the Franciscans and his excommunication by the new Pope, Alexander VI. On May 24, 1497, he and two companions were hanged and their dead bodies burnt and their ashes carefully gathered and thrown into the Arno lest the city should be polluted by their remains.

The Medici did not return till September 1, 1512. Pietro the Unfortunate had died in 1503 and those who came back were the Cardinal Giovanni, his youngest brother Giuliano, Duke of Nemours and their cousin Giulio who had been brought up in the household with them. They had been youths of eighteen, fifteen and sixteen when they were banished; they returned as men of thirty-six, thirty-three and thirty-four, with enough experience of the world to restore continuity. All laws passed since 1494 were repealed, the Great Council established by Savonarola was abolished and the government was restored on exactly the same lines as in the times of Lorenzo, despite the law of 1495 expressly forbidding this. Their grandfather's speech of forty-six years earlier was not forgotten by his grandsons who showed that they too knew how to conquer by showing that they knew how to forgive. Although they had been in exile for eighteen years, there were no executions, proscriptions or confiscations of property and, except for a few well deserved cases, no banishments.

In 1513, within two days of the twenty-first anniversary of *Il Magnifico's* death, Giovanni was elected Pope. In honour of this crowning event, two great companies combined to stage an unforgettable and (thanks to Vasari) unforgotten pageant. 'The head of one of these companies called 'The Diamond' was Giuliano de' Medici, the Pope's brother and it was so called because the diamond was the device of Lorenzo the Magnificent, his father. That of the other, with 'The Branch' as its device, had Lorenzo, son of Pietro de' Medici, as its head, with a dried laurel branch, with new leaves springing forth, to show the revival of his grandfather's name.' *The Diamond* chose Poliziano's successor as Professor of Greek and Latin at the University of Florence to devise a *Trionfo*. 'He arranged one like those of the Romans, with three beautiful wooden cars richly painted. The first represented Boyhood, with a row of boys; the second was Manhood, with persons who had done great things at that season of life; the third was Old Age, with men who had done great deeds when old. All the characters were most sumptuously dressed.'

When Lorenzo de' Medici, who was twenty-one, head of 'The Branch', saw his uncle Giuliano's offering, he determined to out-strip and ordered six triumphs, double in number to those of 'The Diamond'. 'The first, drawn by oxen draped with grass, represented the Golden Age of Saturn and Janus. At the top of the car were Saturn with the scythe and two-headed Janus holding the keys of the Temple of Peace, with Fury bound at his feet, and many things pertaining to Saturn, beautifully coloured. Six pairs of shepherds accompanied this car dressed in sable and martin's fur, wearing shoes of antique pattern and with garlands on their heads of many kinds of leaves. The second car, drawn by two pairs of oxen draped with rich cloth, with garlands at their heads and large beads hanging from their gilt horns, carried Numa Pompilius, second King of the Romans, with the books on religion and all the priestly trappings and necessities for sacrifice, as he was the first of the Romans to regulate sacrifices. Six priests accompanied the car on handsome mules. They wore ancient sacerdotal vestments, with rich gold borders and fringes, some carrying a censer. The third car represented the consulship of Titus Manlius Torquatus, consul after the end of the first Carthaginian war, who governed so that Rome could flourish in virtue and prosperity. This car was drawn by eight fine horses, preceded by six pairs of senators on horseback in togas, accompanied by lictors with the fasces, axes and other instruments of justice. The fourth car, drawn by buffaloes dressed as elephants, represented

Julius Caesar triumphing for his victory over Cleopatra on a car painted with his most famous deeds. The fifth car, drawn by winged horses like griffins, had Augustus, the ruler of the universe, accompanied by six pairs of poets on horseback, crowned like Caesar with laurel and dressed according to their provinces. Each poet bore a scroll inscribed with his name. On the sixth car, drawn by six pairs of heifers richly caparisoned, was the just Emperor Trajan, before whose car rode six pairs of doctors of law.

'After them came the Car of the Golden Age, richly made with many figures in relief and beautiful paintings, among which the four Cardinal Virtues were much admired. In the midst of the car was a great globe, upon which lay a man as if dead, his armour rusted, his back open and emerging therefrom a naked gilded child, representing the Golden Age revived by the creation of Cardinal Giovanni de' Medici Pope Leo X and the end of the Iron Age from which it issued. The dried branch putting forth new leaves had the same signification.

'The gilded boy, the child of a baker who had been paid ten crowns (*scudi*), died soon afterwards from the effects.'

The Pageant of the Golden Age may stand, even in Vasari's matter-of-fact account of it, as a symbolic epitome of the achievement of Lorenzo the Magnificent. But it has, in fact, an enduring relevance of another kind. For the designers of the great 'Triumph' – *Il Magnifico*'s son, Giuliano, and his grandson, Lorenzo, Duke of Urbino, the heads of 'The Diamond' and 'The Branch' – were destined to occupy the two tombs which Michelangelo designed for the New Sacristy of San Lorenzo.

It has been bitterly said that 'among all the splendour and greatness to which the Medici ultimately rose, none of them seems to have thought of raising a monument to the greatest man of the family, though the greatest sculptor of the age helped to immortalise on their tombs two of its insignificant members.' Yet, though no one would question the insignificance of the Giuliano and the Lorenzo memorialised on the New Sacristy tombs, the former idealised as The Man of Action (*L'Azione*) with Night and Day at his feet, the latter as The Man of Thought (*Il Penseroso*) with Dusk and Dawn below him, there is caught there something of *Il Magnifico*'s spirit, even though his body is elsewhere. For Lorenzo the Magnificent was buried in the fine porphyry tomb which he and his brother Giuliano had had made for their father Piero the Gouty and his brother, Giovanni, and in which, later, the murdered Giuliano had also been buried.

Shortly before the death of Pope Leo X in 1521, Michelangelo was commissioned to design a New Sacristy for the Church of San Lorenzo, a Medici Chapel to hold four tombs, those of the great Lorenzo and his brother Giuliano, as well as those of the 'little' Lorenzo, Duke of Urbino, and the

Left: *Giuliano de' Medici, Lorenzo's son: portrait by Bronzino*. Right: *Giovanni de' Medici, Lorenzo's son, in his Papal robes: portrait by Raphael*.

'little' Giuliano, Duke of Nemours, who had recently died. 'I went to Carrara,' the sculptor noted in the April of 1521, 'stayed twenty days, took down all the measurements for the four tombs in clay and drew them on paper.'

Work began in earnest when Giulio de' Medici became Pope Clement VII and on January 12, 1524, Michelangelo recorded, 'Bastiano the carpenter began working with me on the models for the tombs.'

It was then discovered that the dimensions of the New Sacristy made it impossible to accommodate four monumental tombs and – incredibly as it might seem to anyone unacquainted with the character of Pope Clement VII – the two chosen for inclusion were not the great Lorenzo and the almost legendary Giuliano but their nondescript namesakes.

The problem which faced Michelangelo, occupying him till he left

Florence for ever in 1534 was how, despite the restriction, to make the chapel a memorial to the Magnificent. In the first place, he took care to ensure that the figures on the tombs were quite unlike their subjects. Both Giuliano, Duke of Nemours, and Lorenzo, Duke of Urbino, had beards, adopted in deference to the French and, largely for that reason, resented by the patriotic Florentines. Neither of Michelangelo's statues has a beard. And when it was pointed out to him that the figures bore not the faintest resemblance to the men they were supposed to represent, Michelangelo contemptuously asked who was likely to know a thousand years later. Meanwhile, he gave the sculpting of the saints Cosmas and Damian each side of the statue of the Madonna and Child to somewhat pedestrian assistants and lavished his own genius on her, at whom both Lorenzo and Giuliano were made to gaze.

Not till 1559 were the bodies of Lorenzo the Magnificent and his brother brought into the New Sacristy and deposited in an unnamed tomb under the statue of the Madonna. Michelangelo, then eighty-four years old, did not visit Florence for the occasion though the head of the Medici of the time did his best to persuade him to.

With these somewhat unedifying facts in mind, one is in a better position to appreciate Michelangelo's masterpiece of the New Sacristy, the two tombs 'which are probably the best known tombs of any in Europe' and which contrive to honour *Il Magnifico* who should be but is not there.

The Medici Chapel, to give the mausoleum the name by which it is usually known, is the tribute of love, the love of one genius for another. For his formative years from thirteen to seventeen, the younger had been dominated, trained and cared for by the elder with whom he lived and from whom he was inseparable. The twenty-six years which separated Michelangelo from Lorenzo were, considering the time and the circumstances, of little account. The boy, with the blessing of Poliziano (who suggested to him as a subject a battle of centaurs which remains 'technically one of the most amazing works in the history of art') grew up in constant contact with the other arts and with the minds not only of Lorenzo and Poliziano as poets, but of Marsilio, Landino and della Mirandola as philosophers and classicists. He took part in the annual enactment of the *Symposium* by the Platonic Academy and also entertained them by reading aloud modern poetry in his strong Tuscan accent.

The morning Lorenzo died, Michelangelo left his room in the palace and, leaving behind him the prized violet mantle which was one of Lorenzo's gifts to him, returned to his father's house. For weeks he, who could not endure idleness, found that he could do nothing but give way to his sorrow and depression. Eventually he roused himself by spending his savings in buying 'for a modest sum' a block of marble which had long remained exposed to the elements. This he fashioned, at the classical Poliziano's sympathetic suggestion, into a Hercules, Protector of Florence. This, the first of Michelangelo's heroic statues, is now lost (it was last seen in France in the eighteenth century), but it must surely have been Michelangelo's true tribute to his incomparable protector, Lorenzo.

That November the sculptor was invited – or ordered – to the Medici palace once more by Pietro the Unfortunate (whose son, Lorenzo, the subject of the New Sacristy tomb, was born that year), because of a very heavy fall of snow. On such occasions, it was customary to set up huge snow figures outside the churches and palaces of the town and Michelangelo's snowman, whatever it may have been, was set up in the courtyard of the Palazzo Medici.

The circumstances, however, were such that a return to serve *Il Magnifico's* heir was impossible and Michelangelo returned the insult by spreading it abroad that the new head of the Medici took pride in being served by two extraordinary men – himself and a Spanish sprinter whom Pietro could not overtake even on horseback.

The rift became final when, two days before Pietro rode out to welcome Charles VIII, Michelangelo fled from Florence, without telling even his father, and took the road to Rome. The reason, as he himself explained later, was that he had had a vision of Lorenzo in a black, tattered robe who, in great distress, asked him to visit Careggi to warn Pietro that unless he mended his behaviour he would be banished. Michelangelo obeyed, only to be met with Pietro's laughter, and, with the bitter realisation that all that Lorenzo had done was being betrayed by his unworthy son, left Florence and spent the next five years in Rome.

Over twenty years later, a life-battered man in his fifties acknowledged as the pre-eminent painter and sculptor of Italy, he began work on the Sacristy in Florence to commemorate the lord of his youth. As we have seen he was careful to make it plain that the figures on the tombs had no relation to the young Medici buried there. As one writer has put it, 'in each case the subject is of no importance and distorted out of all resemblance to its character.' This is true of even 'symbolic' resemblance, though art critics are apt to insist that The Thinker is an excellent guise for the dissolute libertine who died insane from his excesses at the age of twenty-seven, the most worthless of the family on whose name he had brought nothing but discredit; and that The Man of Action suits the quiet and charming Papal Generalissimo who cared only for the satisfactions of private life, literature and the company of learned men.'

What, then, did Michelangelo intend? Surely that the sculptures represent two aspects of Lorenzo the Magnificent. One clue seems to me the circumstance that the elbow of The Thinker is resting nonchalantly on a small money-box with the hideous head of a bat. This is, indeed, how Lorenzo in those last days when Michelangelo lived with him saw the Medici wealth.

And why have the two men only one helmet and that one of strange, individualistic design worn by The Thinker not by The Man of Action? So questions may continue, all suggesting the same answer, more particularly if the figures of Dawn and Dusk, Day and Night, rich with symbolism, which lie at their feet, are taken into consideration.

Michelangelo's own mood in regard to them we know. When an admirer wrote of Night that 'the Night which you see sleeping so gracefully was wrought in stone by an angel; though asleep she is living; rouse her if you doubt it and she will speak to you.' Michelangelo, in her name replied, using one of Lorenzo's favourite metres:

> *Grato mi e il sonno, e piu l'esser di sasso*
> *Mentre che il danno e la vergogna dura,*
> *Non veder, non sentir, m'e gran ventura*
> *Pero non mi destar : deh parlo basso.*

'Sweet is sleep to me and even more to be of stone, while wrong and shame endure. To be without sight or sense is a most happy chance for me, therefore do not rouse me. Hush! speak low.' A thought echoed superbly by another classical humanist, A. E. Housman:

> Ay, look: high heaven and earth ail from their prime foundation;
>   All thoughts to rive the heart are here and all are vain;
> Horror and scorn and hate and fear and indignation –
>   Oh, why did I awake? When shall I sleep again?

But that was neither the last nor the determining word.

The chapel Michelangelo made for Lorenzo was dedicated to The Resurrection.

London
The Feast of St Antoninus 1973

Opposite: *Michelangelo's* The Thinker *on the tomb of the Duke of Urbino in the Medici Chapel, which may be an idealisation of Lorenzo the Magnificent.*

281

Short Bibliography

A. Fabroni: *Laurentii Medicis Vita* 2 vols. Pisa 1784.

William Roscoe: *The Life of Lorenzo de' Medici* London 1796.

A. von Reumont: *Lorenzo dei Medici* 2 vols. Bonn 1874 trs. Robert Harrison London 1876

E. Armstrong: *Lorenzo de' Medici* (Heroes of the Nations Series) London 1896

E. L. S. Horsburgh: *Lorenzo the Magnificent* London 1905.

C. M. Ady: *Lorenzo dei Medici* (Teach Yourself History Series) London 1955.

J. Burckhardt: *The Civilization of the Renaissance* 1860 trs. 1878 2 vols.

J. A. Symonds: *The Renaissance in Italy* London 1881.

G. Vasari: *The Lives of the Painters, Sculptors and Architects* Florence 1550; English trs. by Hinds, 1900; now in Everyman's Library: 4 vols.

E. Wind: *Pagan Mysteries in the Renaissance* London 1958.

Lorenzo's own works are published in two volumes: *Opere*, ed. Sismondi, Bari 1913.

Some of his poems, including *Ambra* and *La Caccia cal Falcone* are included in Roscoe's biography.

Index

Acknowledgments

The Publishers wish to express their thanks to the following museums, libraries, and other institutions from whose collections works have been reproduced:

Accademia Carrara, Bergamo: 172; Archivio di Stato, Siena: 189; Biblioteca Medicea Laurenziana, Florence: 94, 107, 112, 170, 208; Biblioteca Nazionale Centrale, Florence: 89, 108–109, 111, 149, 239, 245; Biblioteca Nazionale, Naples: 201; Bibliothèque nationale, Paris: 176, 182, 186; Casa Buonarroti, Florence: 269; Fitzwilliam Museum, Cambridge: 258; Galleria Corsino, Florence: 250–251; Galleria degli Uffizi, Florence: 27, 34, 47, 69, 78–79, 80, 82, 97, 143, 154, 158, 190, 277; Galleria dell'Accademia, Florence: 98–99, 100; Galleria Nazionale delle Marche, Urbino: 184; Làndesmuseum, Hannover: 193; Maurits- huis Museum, The Hague: 236; Musée Condé, Chantilly: 153; Musée Bonnat, Bayonne: 175; Museo degli Argenti, Palazzo Pitti, Florence: 75, 263, 265; Museo dell'Opera del Duomo, Florence: 169; Museo del Palazzo Ducale, Mantua: 122–123; Museo di San Marco, Florence: 154; Museo di San Martino, Naples: 194–195; Museo Mediceo, Palazzo Medici-Riccardi, Florence: 31, 38, 50, 163, 207, 267, 272, 273, 277; Museo Nazionale di Bargello: 20, 28, 40, 41, 56, 57, 74, 90, 147, 173, 227, 232, 247, 257; Museum of Art, Cleveland, L. E. Holden Collection: 22–23; National Gallery, London: 36, 119, 150–151, 193, 252, 255; National Gallery of Art, Washington, Samuel H. Kress Collection: 139; Palazzo Vecchio, Florence: 44–45, 54–55, 72–73, 140–141, 201, 217, 228–229, 230–231.

Jacket: Galleria degli Uffizi, Florence.

All photographs reproduced, with the exception of those listed below, are from the Park and Roche Establishment archives (photographers: R. Bencini, M. Carrieri).

Alinari, Florence: 41, 70, 74, 90, 204, 227, 247; Giraudon, Paris: 153, 175, 182; John Freeman, London: 258; Mansell Collection, London: 38, 121, 192, 199, 241; National Gallery, London: 119, 150–151, 193, 252, 255; National Gallery, Washington: 139; Radio Times Hulton Picture Library, London: 192; Scala, Florence: 32–33, 62–63, 78–79, 98–99, 100, 125, 154, 163, 164, 190, 207, 208, 249.